ON THE VERGE

OR
THE GEOGRAPHY
OF YEARNING

Eric Overmyer

BROADWAY PLAY PUBLISHING INC
56 E 81st St., NY NY 10028-0202
212 772-8334 fax: 212 772-8358
http://www.BroadwayPlayPubl.com

First printing: November 1986
Second printing: January 1988
Third printing: June 1990
Fourth printing: May 1994
Fifth printing: December 2000

I S B N: 0-88145-046-4

Book design: Marie Donovan
Word processing: Microsoft Word for Windows
Play text set in Aster y Techna-Type, York PA
Printed on recycled acid-free paper and bound in the U S A

THE PLAYS OF ERIC OVERMYER

NATIVE SPEECH (1984)
ON THE VERGE (1986)
IN PERPETUITY THROUGHOUT THE UNIVERSE
(1989)
IN A PIG'S VALISE (1989)
MI VIDA LOCA (1991)
DARK RAPTURE (1993)
DON QUIXOTE DE LA JOLLA (1993)
THE HELIOTROPE BOUQUET BY SCOTT JOPLIN
AND LOUIS CHAUVIN (1993)
AMPHITRYON (1995, *adaptation*)
FIGARO/FIGARO (1996, *adaptation*)
ALKI (1996)

On the Verge
Is dedicated to
Arnold Cooper
On the occasion of his sixtieth birthday

On The Verge (or *The Geography Of Yearning*) received its professional premiere on January 5, 1985 at Center Stage, Baltimore, Stan Wojewodski, Artistic Director, Peter Culman, Managing Director. The production was directed by Jackson Phippin, with the following cast:

MARY	Mary Layne
FANNY	Brenda Wehle
ALEX	Marek Johnson
GROVER et al.	James McDonnell

The sets were by Tony Straiges, lights by James F. Ingalls, costumes by Del Risberg, sound and music by Paul Sullivan and Janet Kalas, and props by Susan Andrews and Barbara Robinson.

The play begins in 1888.
In Terra Incognita.

Perhaps the imagination is on the verge
of recovering its rights.

ANDRÉ BRETON
(paraphrased by E.O.)

FANNY
MARY
ALEXANDRA
GROVER, ALPHONSE, THE GORGE TROLL, THE YETI, GUS, MADAME NHU, MR. COFFEE, and NICKY PARADISE

All three ladies are *adventurers*.

ALPHONSE, GROVER, et al., are played by a single actor.

The ladies are American, and speak a good 19th-century American speech—not British, nor mid-Atlantic.

The ladies are in full Victorian trekking dress, plus practical accessories—pith helmets, etc.

The titles and journal entries separate each scene. The titles of each scene should be conveyed visually, or aurally, by slide, sign, or recording. The titles are essential, and *must* be used.

The Journal Entries are done to the audience as direct address. They are not being written in the moment, but have been composed previously, and are now being shared.

ACT ONE

(1) On the Verge

(*The ladies are in a hot, white light.*)

MARY: Day One. Landfall.

FANNY: Beach.

MARY: Island or continent?

ALEX: Isthmus or archipelago?

FANNY: Beach. Narrow ribbon. Cliff face. Sheer. Beyond—?

ALEX: Up and over—?

FANNY: Unbearable anticipation.

MARY: Mysterious interior.

(*They sigh.*)

MARY: We have reached our embarcadero.

ALEX: Into the unknown.

MARY: 1888. The last undiscovered, unexplored—bit.

ALEX: Of globe.

FANNY: The sudden force of circumstance.

ALEX: An inheritance.

MARY: Money and time. Time and money.

FANNY: Grover said—

MARY: A mandate from the Boston Geo—

FANNY: "Go!"

ALEX: We find ourselves—

FANNY: Up against it—in the Antipodes—

MARY: Latitude 15 degrees south—

FANNY: Of the Equator.

MARY: Longitude 125 degrees west—

FANNY: Of Greenwich.

ALEX: Somewhere east of Australia, and west of Peru.

MARY: Tropics.

FANNY: Should be good anchovy fishing.

MARY: Poised.

FANNY: On the brink.

ALEX: On the beach.

MARY: On the verge.

ALEX: Set to trek.

MARY: Trekking in *Terra Incognita!*

(*They clasp hands.*)

MARY, ALEX, AND FANNY: Terra Incognita!

(MARY *comes down to do her journal entry.*)

> MARY: Before I began my travels in the un-
> charted reaches of the world, an avuncular col-
> league took me aside. "I have heard your
> peregrinations are impelled, in part, by sci-
> entific curiosity," he said. "Allow me to offer
> you some sage counsel. Always take measure-
> ments, young lady. And always take them from
> the adult male." (*Beat*) Sound advice.

(2) Taking Stock—or—on Sartorial Custom, Civil and Savage

MARY: I have always traveled solo hitherto.

FANNY: As have I.

ALEX: As have I.

MARY: Occasionally encountering a sister sojourner on a trek—

FANNY: Pausing briefly for the pro forma cuppa—

ALEX: And then going our separate ways, alone.

MARY: By "alone" you mean of course in the company of dozens of native bearers, beaters, porters, sherpas, and guides.

FANNY: We agreed. No porters.

ALEX: (*Sighs*) No sherpas.

FANNY: You carry what you collect.

(*They begin to do inventory.*)

MARY: Machetes. Three.

FANNY: Umbrellas. A brace.

ALEX: Rope. Some yards.

FANNY: A gross of hand-tinted picture postcards.

MARY: By your own hand, Fanny?

FANNY: I had them fabricated. I anticipate they will not be readily available en route.

ALEX: Imaginative preconceptions of Terra Incognita, Fanny?

FANNY: Preconceptions? Precisely.

ALEX: Are you clairvoyant, Fanny?

FANNY: Look. Generic scenes of general interest. Generic fauna. Generic jungle. Generic bush.

MARY: They will complement our cartography, which is highly speculative and totally fanciful. Ink pens. Journals, hand-sewn and leather-bound.

FANNY: Hand me my toothbrush, won't you?

MARY: Peacock feathers. Beads. Colored glass. Patent medicines. Specimen bags. Lanterns. Butterfly nets. Cello. Ocarina. Mandolin. Rock-climbing apparatus. *Sherry*. A Persian carpet of modest dimension. Parasols. Mosquito netting. Mineral water. Canteens. Water colors. Sketching canvas. Canopy clips. Bamboo staves. Quartz knives. Iodine. Shepherd's pie. Barley sugar. Lemon drops.

FANNY: Pith helmets.

(*She distributes them. They don them ceremoniously, and in unison.*)

MARY: We're not short of pith—that's sure.

(FANNY *pulls out a rhinestoned tiara and blonde wig.*)

FANNY: Whenever I must palaver with pasha or poobah, I don this tonsorial getup. And lay out a formal tea. It never fails to impress.

MARY: I don't wonder.

FANNY: It stands to reason. Savages are naked. For the most part.

ALEX: I for one am impressed. I've a Kodak! (*She rummages.*)

MARY: No, really?

FANNY: Where did you get it?

ALEX: Friends in high places.

FANNY: Show.

(ALEX *shows.*)

FANNY: Is that it? That little box?

ALEX: The film, it's called, captures the image.

FANNY: Oh?

ALEX: Like honey. Insects in amber. Silver nitrate. I have no way of printing the images. That requires a laboratory. Which would have meant porters.

FANNY: We agreed.

ALEX: We did. Fanny—

(FANNY *models tiara and wig.* ALEX *Kodaks her.*)

FANNY: You won't see what you've Kodaked?

ALEX: Not until we return home.

FANNY: How do you know that it works?

ALEX: You just trust. You "click". You store. You protect. You wait.

FANNY: You hope and pray.

ALEX: You trust. Transport. Guard with your very life. Years of deserts, mountains, pagan tribesmen, and inclement weather. Back in civilization, you hand over your nascent images. Have they survived the travails of the trek? Breathless, you await the results of the chemical revelation. With a little luck—voilà! Kodaks! Lovely mementos. And, best of all, incontrovertible proof for posterity. Documentation.

MARY: I wouldn't trust 'em. Misleading. The natives say they steal your spirit.

ALEX: Funny word, native.

MARY: A Kodak is no more the thing itself than an etching. Flat. A shadow. Physical specimens are what count. Hides, horns, and bobtails.

FANNY: We agreed. No porters.

ALEX: Your natives are mistaken. An unseen moment that would have vanished without a trace is brought to light. The spirit is not stolen. It is illuminated.

MARY: Mysticism.

ALEX: Science.

MARY: That's not science, dear. That's engineering. No, Alexandra, we must have something the Boston Geo can lay hands on.

FANNY: You carry what you collect.

MARY: Physical evidence. Not impressions. Not imagery. Not emotion. Objectivity. Not poetry, m'dears. Not romance. You know what I'm saying.

ALEX AND FANNY: Mmmmmmmmmmmmmmmm.

MARY: Shall we saddle up?

(*Something in the sand catches* ALEX's *eye. She uncovers it.*)

ALEX: A glint in the sand.

FANNY: Hooper do!

MARY: An artifact! So soon! This is lucky!

ALEX: Qu'est ce que c'est?

(*She picks up a metal button and hands it to* MARY.)

ALEX: Gloss this.

MARY: Metallic button. Writing. Oh, this is lucky. Latin letters. What a surprise. I'd have thought runes.

FANNY: I'd have thought glyphs. Can you make it out?

MARY: Not English.

FANNY: Phonetically.

MARY: (*Puzzles it out.*) "Hec—kwhod—ont".

FANNY: There's a question mark after it. It's a question.

(*They try various pronunciations and inquisitive inflections.*)

ALL: "Hec—kwhod—ont"? "Hec—kwhod—ont"? "Hec—kwhod—ont"?

FANNY: Pity it's not English.

ALEX: You didn't expect English, did you, Fanny?

MARY: It would not have surprised me. English is everywhere.

FANNY: A good thing, too.

MARY: Is it? English is the vehicle, and its engine is Empire.

FANNY: Stuff.

ALEX: Perhaps we'll find a translator.

MARY: The first of many mysteries!

(ALEX *does her journal entry.*)

> ALEX: I have seen wonders in the Himalayas. Magic. Mystery. In Ladakh, it was a quotidian

trick for the lamas to raise their body temper-
atures by mere mental exertion. Sheer dint of
will. They would sleep all night in snowbanks.
At dawn, they would douse themselves in freez-
ing streams. Then, ice-blue and on the verge of
extinction, they would sit lotus and meditate
ferociously. Instantly, steam would sizzle off
them in clouds, rising past their furrowed
brows. In an hour, their robes would be dry as
toast—and neatly pressed. (*Beat*)

In the blue shadow of Crystal Mountain, I
watched a Bon shaman wrap himself in his
black cape, fold himself thrice, become a giant
origami crow, flap flap flap his wings, rise into
the sky, and fly across the saffron moon. (*Beat*)

In Lhasa, on the bone-white hill of the Potala,
before the lunar congregation of Buddhist
alchemists, I saw the Dalai Lama himself
transmute great buckets of gold coins. (*Beat*)
Into yak butter.

(3) Up and Over

(*The ladies saddle up.*)

MARY: Let us trek.

FANNY: Mary! Alexandra!

ALEX: Ladies! To the wall!

(*They trek.*)

FANNY: Look behind us.

MARY: Is something gaining?

FANNY: In the sand.

ALEX: Ooooo!

MARY: Our footprints.

FANNY: Making our mark.

(*They continue trekking.*)

MARY: (*A deep inhalation*) Salt air always brings out the metaphysician in me.

FANNY: I always leave Grover in Terre Haute. The Antipodes are not the sort of place one should bring a man.

(*They reach the cliff face.* FANNY *eyeballs it.*)

FANNY: Steep.

MARY: Daunting.

FANNY: Truculent.

MARY: Vertiginous.

ALEX: Child's cake.

(*They prepare their ropes.*)

ALEX: Surely you will both agree trousers would be far more practical for scaling this promontory.

MARY: Alexandra, the civilizing mission of Woman is to reduce the amount of masculinity in the world. Not add to it by wearing trousers. The wearing of trousers—by women—leads inexorably to riding astride a horse. Instead of the modest sidesaddle.

FANNY: And encourages the use of the bicycle. Which for women can never be proper.

ALEX: I happen to be a "wheel enthusiast". And I have often worn trousers—out of sight of civilized settlement, to be sure—whilst wheeling. Or riding horseback. *Astride.* Far more comfortable and sensible than sidesaddle.

FANNY: What can one say?

ALEX: Out of sight of sedentary eyes, I whip off my skirt, under which I have worn sturdy trousers, and am set for practical traveling.

FANNY: Alexandra, are you wearing trousers at this moment?

ALEX: Trousers, ladies, are the future!

MARY: Yes, I am constantly told by armchair travelers that I must wear trousers in the jungle, and leave my skirt at home.

FANNY: Men can be soooo trying.

MARY: I pay no heed, and have often had cause to celebrate my independence. One evening in Malaya near dusk, I fell ten feet into a man-eating tiger trap. Found myself nestled on a cathedral of punji sticks. If I had been wearing trousers, I would have been pierced to the core, and done for. Instead, I found myself sitting on a dozen razor-sharp spikes, in comparative comfort.

FANNY: A petticoat is the only thing for punji sticks. A good stiff petticoat is worth its weight in gold. (*Snorts*) Trousers in the tropics!

ALEX: Oh, jungles. In the Himalayas, trousers are de rigueur. Allons!

(ALEX *leads the way. They scale the cliff. Jungle light. Jungle sounds. Dazzled, they survey the surround.*)

ALEX: A jeweled jungle!

(FANNY *comes down to do her journal entry.*)

FANNY: I introduced croquet to the headhunters of the headwaters of the Putamayo. The sport of kings. They loved it. Simply adored the game. Of course, I insisted they use only regulation wooden balls. I would accept no substitutes. The rascals were always batting their latest trophies about. I was strict. They respected me for that.

(4) The Mysterious Interior

ALEX: Terra Incognita!

FANNY: Ooooo. Hooper Do!

MARY: The mysterious interior.

ALEX: Fantastic! A jeweled jungle! I am extruded! I mean ecstatic. Not extruded.

MARY: Ladies, shall we bushwhack?

(*They step forward and bushwack.*)

FANNY: Some years back, while on assignment in the Amazon River Basin, for my favorite tabloid, *True Trek*, my arch nemesis on *The Globetrotteress* reported I had got myself up in male haberdashery.

MARY: Did you sue?

FANNY: Grover sued. I would have had the wretch horsewhipped.

MARY: I would sooner saunter across the Sahara sans sandals than don trousers.

ALEX: Ladies, I am not advocating trousers for general usage. Or polite society. But there are times one simply must—bite the bullet!

MARY: An umbrella comes in handy. In the jungle.

ALEX: Jungle is not my metier.

MARY: We know. Fanny, what thousand and one uses do you find for your umbrella?

FANNY: Prodding the suddenly faint of heart. Marine soundings. Poking hippopotamii. And whacking the recalcitrant croc. Thwack! The Mighty Silurian!

ALEX: What is a Mighty Silurian?

MARY: So Fanny's lurid tabloids call the crocodile.

ALEX: (*Working out a lyric*) Umbrella. Hmmm. Chum. Fella. Drum. Fun. Swa—swa—swa—swa—Swoon! Ta—ta—ta—Typhoon! La la—tropical fever has got me in its mighty thrall.

(*A sudden downpour. The ladies blossom their umbrellas.*)

FANNY: No, dear. There's no protection from a tropical downpour.

ALEX: None?

FANNY: It must be endured.

ALEX: Jungle jungle, what a foreboding—

(*The rain stops.*)

ALEX: —what a mystery. A jeweled jungle!

FANNY: It'll do. Puts one in mind of the great cloud forest of the Orinoco.

MARY: Not annoying! Not annoying at all! (*With great resolve*) Ladies—shall we whack the bush?

(*They start forward, whacking the bush.*)

FANNY: Ah, the familiar chop chop swack swack. Takes me back. The cloud forest of the Orinoco. Now there is a jungle, ladies. Spiders the size of flapjacks! They flop on you out of the trees! You have to get 'em on the fly! Cut 'em in half in mid-air! Thwack! Spider blood splatters!—hello, what's this? Mysteries underfoot.

(FANNY *finds something: An old-fashioned egg beater, slightly rusty. She holds it various ways, rotors it, giggles.*)

FANNY: What do you think it could be?

MARY: A fan. For this glaze of tropical heat.

FANNY: (*Rotors*) Does not generate the slightest breeze.   .

MARY: A talisman.

FANNY: Totem.

MARY: Amulet.

FANNY: Taboo. Alexandra?

(*She hands it to* ALEX, *who turns it beaters-down, and rotors it with resolve.*)

ALEX: Marsupial's unicycle.

(*Hands it to* FANNY, *who puts it in her belt, like a six-shooter.*)

JOURNAL ENTRY:

> MARY: The bane of my many travels in the tropics is a bland, mucilagenous paste called manioc, made from the forlorn and despicable cassava, a tuber of dubious provenance. A vile concoction, manioc tastes, in the best of recipes, like the bottom of a budgie's cage—and is more suited for masonry than human consumption. Manioc is the quintessential native chop, occurring circumglobularly in the tropics. For those with a taste for prussic acid, manioc may be just your cup of tea.

(5) Native Chop

(*The ladies are bushwhacking. Jungle noises all about.*)

ALEX: I am delicious! I mean delirious. Not delicious.

MARY: Ladies! Shall we whack the bush?

(*They start off.* ALEX *pricks herself on a thorn.*)

ALEX: Ow! Ligament, juicy Nordic, quiz!

FANNY: Marvelous strange oaths, Alexandra.

ALEX: These spikey stickers are a bother. Itch! Lasso pork liquor!

MARY: The bush has its logic.

ALEX: Fine. The glacier is my milieu. Give me an ice face, a mountain of howling wind and stone, or an impassable crevasse. Below zero, I'm in my element. Why can't a jungle be more like a park?

FANNY: Regulated undergrowth?

ALEX: Why not? A little order.

MARY: A jungle has its order, of course.

ALEX: Tips for lady travelers? Or just brushing up on your next address to the Boston Geo?

MARY: Don't snip, or snipe. Dear.

FANNY: When I was last at the Explorer's Club, I had the most extraordinary meal. It was written up in *True Trek*.

ALEX: Please, Fanny, not one of those stories.

MARY: This jungle is not so awful. As jungles go, this jungle is not annoying.

ALEX: It is nothing but. It is one annoyance after another.

MARY: It is dry. A dry jungle is a mercy.

ALEX: Mary, it is soggy. It is saturated. I have fungi growing on my corset stays.

MARY: Comparatively dry. As jungles go, this one is almost arid. Oh, I have waded through swamps for hours on end, emerging at last with a frill of leeches around my neck like an astrakhan collar.

ALEX: There are no astrakhan leeches in the Himalayas. No spikey swamp stickers, no mighty silurians—

MARY: But there are abominable snowmen. I've read Fanny's tabloids.

FANNY: Abominable snowman was on the menu when I was last at the Explorers' Club. But I suspect it was yak. They pride themselves on their Native Chop. I always have something outlandish. Thinking about the Explorers' Club whets my appetite. We must stop for refreshment. (*She puts down her pack and rummages, preparing a snack.*) On my last visit, we had bear chops, buffalo hump, glacé bees' knees, and armadillo knuckles. Which I for one never suspected armadillos had. Followed by muckleshoots, sweet and sour zebra, wolverine surprise, porcupine quills à la Louis quatorze, locust liqueur, and the celebrated moose mousse. I hear not a good year for gnu, I said. I'd skip the snake salad, if I were you, my companion replied, and the candied cats' eyes aren't worth a penny postcard home. We both agreed to eschew the jellied viscera.

ALEX: Fanny, you make the gorge rise.

FANNY: The Explorers are famous for their grubs. Their motto: Grubs from around the globe! And there are always the usual boyish sallies about mighty good grub. Ho ho. Sheer bravado. The Explorers are always throwing up in their top hats at the end of an evening.

MARY: I regret I have never had the pleasure.

FANNY: The grand art of Native Chop is quite impossible to recreate in the effete precincts of civilization.

MARY: Native Chop, in my experience, is inevitably manioc.

FANNY: Always and forever, world without end. Have you ever had manioc fritters?

MARY: No.

FANNY: Not bad. Not good—but not bad.

ALEX: I am famous.

FANNY: Date bread?

MARY: Please.

ALEX: I mean famished. Not famous.

MARY: (*Takes date bread.*) Thank you. This is scrumptious, Fanny.

FANNY: Alex—

ALEX: Thank you. Mmmm, lovely.

MARY: Super, Fanny. Puts manioc to shame.

FANNY: High praise.

MARY: Ubiquitous manioc. We won't escape it. Mark my words. (*Shudders*) Native Chop.

FANNY: This is not Africa, Mary. This is Terra Incognita. Cream cheese?

ALEX: I don't believe I've ever. What is it?

FANNY: Not cream and not cheese, but it's thick and rich and comes in tins.

ALEX: Thick and rich? Like Mrs. Butterworth!

MARY: Who is Mrs. Butterworth?

(*Pause*)

ALEX: Oh. (*Beat*) I don't know.

MARY: I'll hazard some. Looks harmless. Spread it on my date bread. Thank you. Has the same consistency as manioc.

FANNY: Mary!

ALEX: What a treat! Is it new?

FANNY: Invented in Chicago, I believe. Well, everything is. Take the ice cream sandwich.

ALEX: I've never had one. This is rather nice. Where did you get it? Friends in high places? Will it keep?

FANNY: We must devour it immediately. You know, I don't remember packing it. Or buying it for that matter. I didn't make it. I made the date bread.

(*Pause*)

MARY: Another slice, Fanny.

FANNY: You know, only a few days on, and I am desperate for a bath.

MARY: I concur. What is life without a loofah? Look!

(*They peer ahead.*)

ALEX: He's wearing a uniform.

FANNY: What power? Whose sphere of influence is this plateau?

MARY: This is Terra Incognita! A New World. Sans spheres.

FANNY: Manifest Destiny and the American Way are not spheres.

ALEX: (*To herself*) Rhomboids of influence, trapezoids of destiny.

FANNY: We are emissaries, Alexandra, of the good will and benignity of President McKinley. Cleveland. Taft. Whoever is president now. You know. One of those Ohio politicians. Muttonchops.

ALEX: Can you name the vice-president?

FANNY: Not if my life depended on it.

ALEX: Nor I.

MARY: Perhaps he traded for it.

FANNY: The vice-presidency? Of course he traded for it. He's a Democrat. Well? Isn't he?

MARY: No, the native. Perhaps he traded for the uniform.

ALEX: Shall we palaver? He sees us. (*She waves.*)

MARY: I once traded twelve calico blouses to the Masai. Empress sleeves.

ALEX: What did you trade them for?

MARY: My life. White knuckles and chewed nails, dear.

ALEX: (*Dreamily*) The Masai. Sigh.

MARY: When worn by a brawny warrior with nothing—but red paint—and a necklace of leopard tails—(*Beat*) a calico blouse—(*Beat*) is really quite—(*Beat*) fetching.

ALEX: I should think so.

FANNY: I once encountered the Masai. I said: Wow! Wow! Wow!

ALEX: And how did they reply?

MARY: He's approaching.

FANNY: They seemed to like that. Let's set tea. I'll change.

(FANNY *goes off to change.* MARY *and* ALEX *watch the native's approach, as they prepare for tea.*)

ALEX: Funny word, native. Assuming he is a native. Everyone is a native of somewhere, when you think about it. So I guess he must be a native at that. Where are you a native, Mary?

MARY: I haven't a thing to wear. I wish I could wash. Oh, what is life without a loofah!

JOURNAL ENTRY:

> MARY: In Kuala Lumpur, the seraglio of the Sultan was—a honeycomb. It was as many-chambered as the heart of a tribe. I recall the cavernous steam rooms on cold evenings, full of echoing voices and escarpments of mist. The inlaid geometric gold-leaf calligraphy. The rattan sofas. The acres of tile the color of sky. And a sponge conjured from the exoskeleton of an indigenous fruit. The loofah. Loofah—

(6) High Tea—or, Many Parts Are Edible

(*The ladies have set tea.* FANNY *has donned not only her wig and tiara, but an elaborate rhinestoned gown. Their guest,* ALPHONSE, *wears an impeccable German airman's uniform, and speaks with an extravagant German accent.*)

ALEX: Loofah. Loofah. Now there's a word to conjure with! Powerful juju.

FANNY: More date bread?

ALPHONSE: Oh zank you zo much.

FANNY: Another cup of tea?

ALPHONSE: No, zank you. Mein kidneys are floatingk. Heh heh.

ALEX: Are you a native?

ALPHONSE: Zorry?

ALEX: You don't mind my asking.

ALPHONSE: Nein.

MARY: If you don't mind my saying so, Mr. Bismark—

ALPHONSE: Please. Call me Alphonse.

MARY: Alphonse. If you don't mind my saying so, you sound a trifle German.

ALPHONSE: Alsace-Lorraine.

ALEX: Fascinating.

FANNY: How do you happen to find yourself here?

MARY: Is Alsace-Lorraine French or German these days?

ALPHONSE: Gut qvestion. Geography iz deztiny, ladies!

ALEX: Oh, that's good! I'll make a note of it.

MARY: Alphonse, sprechen sie Deutsch, s'il vous plait?

ALPHONSE: Nein. I never haf been dere.

FANNY: How do you happen to find yourself in this country, did you say?

ALPHONSE: I am a native.

ALEX: This is not Alsace-Lorraine—am I wrong?

ALPHONSE: I never haf been dere. I haf not der foggiest notion vich vay Alsace-Lorraine iz. Schtraight up in der air, vy not, eh?

MARY: Forgive me, but I don't follow.

ALPHONSE: He vas! Him. Not me. No! No! No! No eat! No eat! No eat Alphonse! No eat Alphonse! I am varningk you! I am schtringy! No eat Alphonse! Aaaaaiiiieeeeeeeeeeee!

(*A stricken pause*)

FANNY: I no savvy, as they say out west in Indian Territory. What is this fellow's problem?

MARY: He is not Alphonse from Alsace-Lorraine.

ALPHONSE: No vay, José. I'm from right here at home. Dat vas him. Alphonse. Der von I ate. His uniform, his accent. His syntax. Zide effects. Occupational hazard. Hoppens everytime I eat schomevon.

FANNY: Oh, goodness.

ALPHONSE: I should schtick to date bread. Delicious. (*He has another slice.*)

ALEX: He's a cannibal.

FANNY: Now that's really native chop.

MARY: Nothing to be alarmed about. Cannibals are perfectly rational human beings.

FANNY: You are a liberal, Mary.

MARY: I am an anthropologist. I traveled extensively amongst the Indigos. Cannibals—but lively. Anthropophagii tend to be sluggish, you know. I found them no bother to me at all. Of course, you had to keep them from eating your porters. Frequent head counts were the order of the day. There are two sorts of folks in the world. The sort you drink with, and the sort you eat with. Cannibals you drink with.

ALPHONSE: Ja! I am a Free Mason! (*Pause*) Or, radder, that little rascal Alphonse vas a Free Mason. Egxcuze me, ladies, I am, at der moment, a little confuzed. Too zoon after zupper.

MARY: A Free Mason. What else do you know about your—about Alphonse.

ALPHONSE: He vas a pilot.

FANNY: A riverboat?

ALPHONSE: Nein, nein, nein. He flew. May I have some more of zis date bread, pliz? Und creamcheese? Good schtuff, zis creamcheese.

MARY: You were saying, Alphonse?

ALPHONSE: I vas sayingk, I vas sayingk, ja, um, I vas,

he vas, ve vas, whoever ve vas now, ve vere a pilot.
Of a flyingk machine.

FANNY: Nonsense.

ALPHONSE: Ja, you betcha. Heavier dan der air. A
dirigible.

MARY: A dirigible.

ALPHONSE: Ja. Dirigible.

FANNY: A dirigible.

ALEX: Dirigible.

ALPHONSE: Dirigible, ja, dirigible.

MARY: What is a dirigible? Alphonse?

ALEX: What a succulent word! Dirigible, dirigible,
dirigible. Dirigible. Dirigible.

MARY: Alex!

ALEX: Up your old dirigible. Give us your huddled
dirigibles, yearning to breathe free. Have a dirigible
on me, big fella. One mint dirigible to go.

(*A pause.* ALPHONSE *regards* ALEX *askance.*)

ALPHONSE: Vell, it's a balloon.

MARY: Hot air?

ALPHONSE: Inert gazz.

ALEX: Inelegible dirigible. Illegible dirigible. Incor-
rigible dirigible. Gerbil in a dirigible! I'll wager it's
one of those words which has no true rhyme in English. Of course, it's not an English word, is it?

FANNY: You must explain your obsession with rhyme.
It borders on the unhealthy. I've read that preoccu-
pation with rhyme is one of the symptoms of incipient
hysteria.

ALEX: Knackwurst!

MARY: What happened to the dirigible, Alphonse?

ALPHONSE: Schtill dere, as far as I know. You vant a look, cuties?

FANNY: You, sir, are growing impertinent.

ALPHONSE: Zay, dat's a nice vig you got dere. Mein zizter haz a vig like dat.

FANNY: Does she enjoy it?

ALPHONSE: She lofs it! A lot!

MARY: How do we locate your dirigible?

ALPHONSE: Follow der yellow brick road, shveeties.

MARY: Sorry?

ALPHONSE: Take der segund egxit. Vatch for der Burma Shave signs. Oh, buoy. I should never had taken dat exxtra schlice of date bread. Never eat on a full schtomach.

MARY: Alphonse—

ALPHONSE: Egxcuze me, ladies. Zank you for der chow. You must come to eat viz me shomeday. I make a mean manioc strudel.

ALEX: Manioc, my favorite.

FANNY: Have you ever had manioc fritters?

ALPHONSE: Ve vill haf to trade recipes.

MARY: Alphonse, couldn't you see your way clear to guide us to the dirigible? We'll pay wages.

ALPHONSE: Zorry. I am not vell. I haf to get zis Alphonse out of mein zyztem. Perhops ve meet again, mein blue angels. Vaya con Dios!

MARY: Auf wiedersehn.

ALPHONSE: (*He hands* FANNY *a bundle.*) A token of mein steam. Big juju. Lof dat vig. (*He exits.*)

FANNY: His steam, indeed.

(*She unwraps it. It's another egg beater, a rather different model.* FANNY *hands it to* ALEX.)

FANNY: I've already got one.

ALEX: Thank you so much. I'll keep it with me always.

(*They rotor at one another and laugh.*)

MARY: A cannibal from Alsace-Lorraine. Will wonders never cease?

FANNY: Yes, Mary, there are two sorts of people in the world. There are cannibals—and there are lunch.

MARY: Fanny, you are a Social Darwinist.

ALEX: What do you suppose he meant by Burma Shave?

FANNY: I've been to Burma.

MARY: As have I.

ALEX: (*With sudden fierce conviction*) There are no cannibals in Tibet! No matter what the Red Chinese claim!

(*Pause*)

MARY AND FANNY: What on Earth is a Red Chinese?

JOURNAL ENTRY:

> MARY: By and large the company has been charming. As a confirmed-since-childhood solo sojourner, I am astonished. Perhaps I have overvalued the pleasures of solitude heretofore. (*Takes a deep breath.*) I feel the rare air of Terra Incognita working its way upon me like acid on an old coin, the tarnish of the past dissolving in a solvent of iridescent light. I tingle. Objects shimmer on the horizon. At sunset, a tantalizing mist, a web, a membrane envelopes us.

(7) Ember Tales

(*Twilight descends. A campfire. The ladies are telling tales.*)

MARY: There is nothing so fascinating as fire.

FANNY: When I was sleeping in a rice paddy under a blood moon, near the Irriwaddy River Delta, I awoke to find myself surrounded. By a band of cut-throat dacoits. Thuggees. Brigands. Buccaneers. They wore turbans with rubies set in the brow, and bejeweled daggers. And they were led by a woman—a Bandit Queen! She was a devotee of Kali, the Goddess of Death!

ALEX: I am often asked about Tibetan cuisine. In Lamdo, I apprenticed myself to a sorcerer. My mentor had quarrelled with a rival shaman. A blood feud. One morning, Master Dzo baked two great cakes of ground millet. He baked them flat as platters and hard as wheels. When the cakes were cool, he spun them into the sky. Hurled them, as though they were discuses. They spun and spun, rising in the sky, sailing over the city until they searched out the stone hut of the second sorcerer. The cakes whirled like saw blades, swooped down, and sliced the hut in half. Battered it to crumbs. (*Beat*) I think that sums up Tibetan cuisine. It is not haute.

FANNY: While travelling in the Rocky Mountains some years back, I repelled a rabid drooling grizzly bear with a series of piercing yodels. (*She demonstrates: three bloodcurdling yodels.*)

MARY: That reminds me of my father, who was a famous pharmacist.

ALEX: Did your father yodel, Mary?

MARY: No. He invented a tonic for catarrh.

ALEX: After an hour, their robes would be dry as toast. And neatly pressed. Extraordinary visages. They would *concentrate.*

FANNY: I once encountered the Masai. I said— "Wow"!

MARY: Talking drums always bring out the Neolithic Man in me.

(*Pause*)

(FANNY, *reflecting on the Masai, silently mouthes a "Wow!" The ladies settle in for the night.*)

(FANNY *does her journal entry.*)

> FANNY: Dear Grover. We had lunch today—or was it yesterday—with the most amicable cannibal. He admired my wig. The tabloids will feast. I can hear *The Globetrotteress* licking her chops now. "Fanny's Cannibal—Discovers Maneating Balloonist in Darkest Antipodes— Boston Geo Views Claim Warily." The jaundice of yellow journalism. One more card in the catalogue my critics are fond of calling Fanny's Follies. (*Beat*) Terra Incognita exhilarates. Intoxicates. There is an hallucinatory spiciness to the air. We are in the grip of a communal fever dream. Alex mutters continually about the "Red Chinese", and Mary makes reference to an anthropological penny-dreadful entitled *The Naked and the Dead*. Myself, I dream about mysterious machinery, discover strange objects in my baggage, and strange phrases in my mouth: "Air-mail." "Blue-sky ventures." "So long."

(8) An Apparition

(*The ladies are sleeping around the fire.* FANNY *snores, a ferocious sound. A figure appears on the edge of the light:* GROVER, FANNY's *husband, a prosperous Mid-West broker. He is wearing a large black oval carved African mask. He listens to* FANNY *snore. Scratches his eyebrow. Growls softly.* FANNY *awakes with a start.*)

FANNY: What? Who? (*Looks closer. Mouthes a silent "Wow!" She gets up and approaches him.*) I have no calico blouses, but I will trade you cream cheese. It is not bad. Not manioc, but not bad.

(GROVER *chuckles.* FANNY *examines* GROVER's *suit and shoes.*)

FANNY: Are you or are you not Masai?

GROVER: I'm just your grizz-a-ly bear, Fanny. (*Taking off mask.*) What a snore, Fanny. You'll keep the leopards away.

FANNY: Grover!

GROVER: Don't be cross.

FANNY: Why shouldn't I be? Bother a body in the middle of the night. In the middle of the jungle.

GROVER: I came to give you a message.

FANNY: I'm all ears.

GROVER: Don't speculate on the future.

(*Pause*)

FANNY: Your mother warned me you were hermetic.

GROVER: I also wanted to say goodbye.

FANNY: Grover, we said goodbye. In Terre Haute. Some months ago. Are you staying dry?

GROVER: Dry as toast. Well, Fanny. I had something up my sleeve for Arbor Day next. It was—sorta special. Yikes. Well, Fanny. Goodnight.

FANNY: Goodnight, Grover. Are those new shoes?

GROVER: Don't forget to write.

FANNY: Do I ever?

GROVER: You are a faithful correspondent, Fanny. Goodbye.

(*He disappears.* FANNY *stares after him. Shivers a little.* ALEX *wakes, gets up, goes to* FANNY, *and taps her on the shoulder. She starts.*)

FANNY: Oh!

ALEX: Fanny—are you a somnambulist?

FANNY: What? Oh, I must be. Fancy that.

ALEX: Come back to the fire.

(ALEX *returns to the fire.*)

FANNY: I have had the most vivid dream.

(MARY *arises and does her journal entry.*)

> MARY: At dawn and dusk, the essence of the
> jungle increases a hundredfold. The air be-
> comes heavy with perfume. It throbs with un-
> seen presence. A savage tapestry of squawks,
> cries, and caws presses upon one with an al-
> most palpable pressure. A cacophonous echo-
> lalia—snarling, sinister menace—as though
> the sound of the jungle itself could tear one
> limb from limb.

(9) Fort Apache

(*Dawn breaks. Jungle noises. The ladies break camp. The
ladies travel. Jungle noises all about. The ladies are alert,
cautious.*

Suspenseful.

*The jungle noises increase in ferocity. They become men-
acing.*

*The ladies draw and open their umbrellas. They form a
defensive triangle, shoulder to shoulder.*

The jungle noises attack, snarl, and snap.

*The ladies fend off the jungle noises with their umbrellas,
fencing and jabbing sharply.*

The umbrellas blossom.

*The ladies rotate across the stage, a vanquishing star,
scattering the jungle noises, which howl and flee.*

The ladies lower their umbrellas. They celebrate quietly.)

JOURNAL ENTRY:

ALEX: Funny word, native. Native. Native. (*She Kodaks an imaginary native.*) Image. Native. Image-native. Imaginative. I am a native of the image. An indigine of the imagination. Gone native. Renegade. Commanchero.

(10) In the Jungle—The Mighty Jungle

(*The ladies bushwhack through a swamp.*)

ALEX: Ooo, ow, natter blast! Savage sour lichtenstein! Lactating minuet! This jungle exhausts me! Surely you must agree trousers would be far and away more practical for this primeval muck.

MARY: On the contrary, Alexandra. One evening near dusk, as we were negotiating the treacherous Black Quicksands of Baluchistan, I slipped off solid ground, and found myself sinking into infinite bog. Fortunately, my sturdy skirt ballooned around me, held its shape, and kept me buoyant until assistance arrived. A few moments later, I lost half a dozen porters in the blink of an eye. Sucked under the sands, like that! Fooop! Poor men weren't wearing skirts.

ALEX: Ah! Look!

(*Sound of a croc.* FANNY *vanquishes it.*)

FANNY: The Mighty Silurian! Thwack!

(*The ladies reach solid ground.*)

MARY: Time for a nose powder.

FANNY: I could do with a bit of a primp.

ALEX: I'll follow suit.

(*They pull beaded handbags from their packs, move some distance through the jungle, and freshen up.*)

MARY: In the Congo, I was known as Only Me.

ALEX: Only Me?

MARY: I would enter a village or burst into a clearing or emerge from the bush shouting, "It's only me, it's only me!"

FANNY: Immediately disarming the hostile natives, who naturally enough spoke English.

MARY: Dear Fanny. Tone of voice is everything.

FANNY: I was known as Bébé Bwana.

ALEX: Bébé?

FANNY: It's difficult to explain. Out of context.

MARY: I never got over being called "Sir."

ALEX: Nor I.

FANNY: Nor I.

MARY: Human once more.

FANNY: I am revivified.

ALEX: I am refurbished. I mean refreshed. Not refurbished. Ah! Feel that breeze, ladies!

(*The wind comes up. The ladies prepare for cold weather, donning scarves, goggles, etc.*)

JOURNAL ENTRY:

FANNY: I felt as though I were a prisoner in a kaleidescope.

(11) A Prisoner in a Kaleidescope

(*The wind comes up. They move across the stage. The wind whistles. They stop.*)

FANNY: Alexandra. Here's your howling ice field.

ALEXANDRA: My forte. Allons!

(*They cross the ice field in slow motion. The invisible rope between them breaks, and they begin twirling slowly over the ice, in different directions, away from one*

another, toward the edges, in silence. At the brink, they
stop. Teeter. Freeze. Relax. They catch their breath.)

MARY: A narrow one—

ALEX: Whoo whistle lug—

FANNY: A scrape—

(*Relieved laughter. They make their way carefully to the*
center and one another.)

MARY: What happened, did the rope—

ALEX: The rope—

FANNY: It snapped, I felt it go—

ALEX: Broke—

MARY: Spinning like a gyro—

ALEX: Spinning—

MARY: Graceful, I was so—

FANNY: So—

MARY: Calm—

FANNY: Calm, yes—

FANNY AND MARY: Calm—

FANNY: Eeerily calm—

ALEX: Spinning toward the lip of the void—

MARY: My mind clear—

ALEX: Into the infinite cerulean—

MARY: I thought of my father, the famous
pharmacist—

ALEX: Did your life, you know, flash before you?

MARY: Too dizzy, my dear—

ALEX: They say drowning sailors—

MARY: No, just him.

FANNY: I felt as though I were a prisoner in a
kaleidescope.

ALEX: Oh, Fanny, that's good.

MARY: A book title. I'd make a note of it.

(FANNY *does. They sigh.*)

ALEX: Whew, lacerated fingerbowl!

MARY: Fingerbowl, indeed! Well said, Alex.

FANNY: A scrape. A palpable scrape.

MARY: Sheer luck, running into that ice wall.

FANNY: Fortuitous.

ALEX: I'm all over bruises in the morning.

(FANNY *is hit by a snowball.*)

FANNY: Alexandra!

ALEX: Yes?

FANNY: High spirits need not always be accompanied by hi-jinks.

ALEX: You always cast your eye upon me because I'm the youngest. But that missile came from over there.

(*They all look. A barrage of snowballs. They dodge.*)

MARY: Oh, dear!

FANNY: Watch yourselves! Oh, Alexandra!

(*Dodging,* ALEX *slips and pratfalls. The breath flies out of her.*)

ALEX: Whomp!

MARY: Are you all right?

(*A yeti appears at the stage edge—a silky mane from head-to-foot.*)

YETI: (*Growls beast language*) ARRGGGGRRRACKAAACK!

MARY: A silkie.

ALEX: (*Picking herself up.*) Silkies are seals, silly. That's a yeti.

YETI: (*Growls beast language*)
LLLLLLLLUUUUUUUURRRRRAAAAAAA-
EEECCCCCKOOO!

ALEX: Oh, yes you are!

YETI: (*Growls beast language*) RASSRASSRASS!

ALEX: Tibet teems with 'em, m'dears. Yes, Fanny's
tabloids call them abominable snowmen.

FANNY: He's not so abominable.

MARY: He's rather adorable.

ALEX: He's smallish, for a yeti.

MARY: He's a baby yeti.

FANNY AND MARY: He's sweet.

(*The ladies chick and coo and gush, luring the yeti closer.
He retreats, terrified.*)

YETI: (*Growls beast language*)
WHHHUUUWHHHAAAASNARP! (*He vanishes.*)

MARY: Oh, dear. Frightened him off.

ALEX: The yeti is shy and elusive. Although his cry is
often human, and tuneful.

(*From offstage:*)

YETI: (*Growls beast language*)
AIIIIIYIIIIIIIYAIIIAIWHA!

FANNY: The little sasquatch has gone for more
snowballs, no doubt. (*She is hit by a snowball.*)
AHHHH!

MARY: Baby yeti may have yeti cronies. I think
prudence dictates we move on.

(*They hike downstage. Peer into a deep gorge.*)

ALEX: Ooo!

FANNY: Precipice.

MARY: Chilling.

ALEX: This gorge is so like the Himalayas!

MARY: There's a bridge. Vines and planks. Shall we risk it?

FANNY: By all means.

(ALEX *takes three Andean breaths.*)

ALEX: Now—this (*Breath*) is (*Breath*) air (*Breath*) ladies!

JOURNAL ENTRY:

FANNY: An awful yawning chasm. An antediluvian suspension.

(12) Not Quite Robert Lowell

(*The ladies are crossing a high gorge on a swaying, single-plank, vine-rope bridge.*)

MARY: "Mysticism and Mesmerism in Madagascar" was a paper I delivered to the Ladies Fetish and Taboo Society of Annapolis. It was a sensation. I followed that with "Tribadism in the Tropics"—which caused quite a stir. Rubbed several spectators the wrong way.

ALEX: What is "tribadism"?

FANNY: (*Knowing exactly what it is*) I'm sure I haven't the least notion.

ALEX: This gorge is so like the Himalayas.

FANNY: I am convinced that the modern craze for anthropology is actually a subterranean sexual inflammation, flimsily got up as scientific curiosity.

ALEX: I am hypnotized.

FANNY: An unhealthy obsession with rites—

ALEX: I mean homesick. Not hypnotized.

FANNY: Mating rites, puberty rites, rites of sacrifice, rites of passage, poly this and poly that and poly the other—

ALEX: Nacho frazzle asterisk! It is so delicious to be out of that leech-infested swelter. Look! (*They turn in the direction* ALEX *points.*) Oh! Dirigible!

MARY: Pilotless. Caroming off the canyon walls.

FANNY: The Flying Dutchman dirigible! What a story for *True Trek*!

(*They have nearly completed their crossing. Their way is blocked by the* GORGE TROLL, *a young man in a leather jacket, blue jeans, t-shirt, and sideburns and greased-back hair.*)

TROLL:
What have we here but travelers three
Comin' cross the bridge to rap with me
In Xanadu said Ka-u-ba-la Khan
Hey there sweet things what's goin' on?

(*Pause*)

FANNY: Alex, I believe verse is your province.

ALEX: You speak English!

TROLL:
This ain't Swahili, I gotta confess
You hearin' more if you talkin' less

FANNY: Swahili seems mathematically more probable than English, my good man. Although I welcome its appearance in this obscure corner of the globe—even in your ghastly patois.

TROLL:
Castigate the way I talk—
I'll agitate the way you walk!

(*He sways the bridge.*)

ALL: Whoooooooo!

MARY: English is the language of Empire, Fanny.

FANNY: I do not wish to embroil us in a political discussion on *the lip of the void*, Mary. Don't you think we ought to seek Terra Firma?

TROLL:
> You may not dig my lingo but I'll settle your hash
> You wanna get by me gotta have some cash

FANNY: I don't believe I savvy.

TROLL:
> This is my bridge, baby, and I'm the Troll
> To step on over you gotta pay the toll.

ALEX: A troll's toll. How droll. He's good. But not quite Robert Lowell.

FANNY: Alex.

ALEX: Whoever he is. Robert Lowell, I mean.

FANNY: This is extortion!

TROLL:
> You want sun sometimes you get rain instead
> If you can't hack it you shoulda stood in bed

MARY: When in Rome.

(*She pays. They cross off.*)

MARY: Baksheesh! In Terra Incognita!

TROLL: Baksheesh-kabob, baby.

ALEX: What's it like, being a troll?

TROLL: Like?

ALEX: How do you find it?

TROLL: This is just my day job.

FANNY: You're not a born-to-the-bridge troll?

TROLL: I'm an actor. I study.

FANNY: Where do you study?

TROLL: At the Studio.

FANNY: That seems reasonable. Have you done Congreve?

TROLL: I don't think so.

FANNY: What have you done?

TROLL: C'mon, I've done it all. "Sense memory," "emotional recall," "private moment"—

MARY: These must be new plays from Terra Incognita. Indigenous drama. How would you characterize "Private Moment"?

TROLL: Intense.

FANNY: You aren't, by any chance, Mr. Coffee?

TROLL: Not the last time I looked. Hey, ladies. Costume drama—get over it. (*To* ALEX) You I like. What about a spin on my chopper?

ALEX: Some other time.

TROLL:
Your loss, angel food.
Ladies, take it light
And everything will be all right.

(*He exits.*)

ALEX: Vaya con Dios!

(*Sound of an enormous unmufflered motorcycle roaring off into the sunset.*)

MARY: I think we must presume English to be the Lingua Franca of Terra Incognita.

FANNY: (*Snorts*) None dare call it English.

MARY: Did you fancy his lyrics, Alexandra?

ALEX: No. But I admired his dedication to his art.

MARY: Irony is not one of your strong suits, is it?

ALEX: What do you mean? I understand that troll! Despite outward appearances, I am an artist, not an intrepid polytopian.

FANNY: Oh, Alex, for goodness sakes, yes you are. You're one of the original polytopians, don't dissemble.

ALEX: Well, yes, I am. High adventure and stupefying risk are my metier. But, ladies—all this rigor and unimaginable hardship, all this uninsurable danger, all this adrenal giddiness, all this oxygen debt and spartan discipline and rude hygiene—all this is mere prelude. A prologue to my brilliant career. I'm not making a life out of all this tramping about, you know. I shall shed my wanderlust like a damp poncho. And become a lyricist. Of popular songs.

FANNY: Victor Herbert quakes.

MARY: I wonder what that conveyance was?

ALEX: He called it a chopper.

FANNY: Loud.

ALEX: (*With sudden conviction*) The future is loud!

JOURNAL ENTRY:

> MARY: I feel a sea change coming over me. A disturbance of my very molecules. As though the chemical composition of my blood has been altered by breathing the rare air of Terra Incognita. I have begun to dream in a new language. My imagination seems to sculpt the landscape. Images flow between the inner and outer worlds, and I can no longer determine their point of origin. I have a growing premonition we are about to pierce the membrane.

(13) Plot Thickener

(*The ladies have moved some distance from the bridge.*)

FANNY: I rather think that Troll is one of the elusive Mole People. The speculative literature on the Antipodes postulates the existence of a subterranean race. Oh, look— (*She has spied a bit of paper caught in a branch. She plucks it.*)

ALEX: Share, Fanny.

FANNY: A clipping. Folded thrice. From *The New York Times*.

MARY: Reputable. Trustworthy.

FANNY: The *Herald-Tribune*, pour moi. This sheds new light. Terra Incognita cannot be utterly benighted if one can get *The New York Times*. (*Studies clipping*) A Kodak of a man. Never heard of this fellow. Behind him an impressive array of snow mountains. His arms are spread—so: (*Imitates a man gesturing about the size of a large fish*.) The caption reads: President Nixon. Grand Tetons. June, 1972. Quote: "I had trout from the lake for dinner last night. They were so good I had them again for breakfast. I haven't had anything but cereal for breakfast since 1953." Endquote.

(*Pause*)

MARY: 1953? 1972?

ALEX: Printer's errors?

MARY: Two such errors in one tiny *Times'* item? Not credible.

FANNY: Dickensian character. Looks like something off the bottom of the sea bed. (*Pause*) President. President Nixon. President of what?

ALEX: Some eating club or other. Where men have breakfast, and compare their trophies.

MARY: No. The United States.

FANNY: How do you know?

MARY: I just know. Don't ask me how.

FANNY: I thought McKinley was President.

MARY: Garfield.

ALEX: Taft, you daft duo.

FANNY: Alexandra, the interjection of song lyrics into otherwise civilized conversation is strictly prohibited.

ALEX: Surely not president of the United States. How could a man who hasn't had an egg for breakfast in twenty years be president of the United States?

FANNY: You know, he rather resembles an orangutan in a dinner jacket.

MARY: I could do with some trout.

ALEX: The Grand Tetons are a lovely little range.

FANNY: Someday they will be preserved as a national park by Teddy Roosevelt.

MARY: Teddy Roosevelt?

ALEX: I've never heard of him.

FANNY: Oh, yes you have. Bully bear and San Juan Hill, and all that.

ALEX: No.

FANNY: His statue is in front of the Museum of Natural History.

MARY: In New York? No. It is not. Not when I was there last.

FANNY: Certainly not. That statue will not be erected until 1936.

(*Pause*)

ALEX: Do you know why there is evil in the world?

FANNY: Metaphysical speculation, Alexandra?

MARY: I don't think so. Do you?

ALEX: Yes, I do.

FANNY: You are so young.

MARY: Why is there evil in the world, Alexandra?

ALEX: To thicken the plot.

(*Pause*)

FANNY: I believe you are exactly right.

(ALEX *seizes the clipping.*)

ALEX: (*Happily*) This is plot thickener!

MARY: Yes!

FANNY: Yes! Ladies, we are in a strange new world.

MARY: Terra Incognita, by definition, could not be otherwise. I have a theory. One that explains the unknown objects. The strange words in our mouths. The references to persons unknown that spring to mind. Spring to mind. It is spring in our minds, ladies. A New World. Blossoming! Within and without! I believe, with each step, each chop of the machete, we are advancing through the wilderness of time as well as space. Chronology as well as geography. Not—as we usually do in savage lands, moving backward into the past, into pre-history—but forward, into the future! A New World, within and without! Beckoning!

(*Pause*)

FANNY: A new world! Within and without!

ALEX: It would explain the dirigible.

FANNY: The clipping from 1972.

ALEX: The Nixon.

MARY: Mrs. Butterworth. Burma Shave. Cream cheese.

ALEX: Robert Lowell. The troll.

FANNY: It would explain why, now, burning in my forebrain like a Mosaic tablet, is the copyright date for a novel entitled *Herzog*.

MARY: Something else is happening, obviously. Something even more astonishing. Not only are we advancing in time, not only are we encountering the future with every step—(*Beat*) Ladies, we are beginning to know the future! (*Beat*) It is entering into our consciousness. Like mustard gas. Whatever that is. Wait a moment. I'll tell you. (*She osmoses.*) Oh. Oh. Oh. Unfortunate simile. I withdraw it.

ALEX: We are absorbing the future! Through osmosis!

FANNY: As long as you're at it, osmos Red Chinese for us.

ALEX: Let me try. (*She osmoses.*) Something's coming in, yes, like a radio transmission. (*She holds up a hand.*) Don't ask. (*She osmoses.*) Hmmmm.

FANNY: Yes?

ALEX: Little Red Book. Great Leap Forward. Swimming the Yang-tze River. Tractor Operas.

FANNY: Operas about tractors?

ALEX: Running dogs. And— (*Osmoses.*) They're friends of Nixon!

(*The ladies leap about excitedly.*)

MARY: Ladies, this is fantastic. I presume you are feeling—with me—slightly tremulous—a bit fluttery around the gills. Ladies, I don't know about you, but I am experiencing a definite, a palpable—yearning for the future!

ALEX: Oh, Mary! Yes! (*Osmoses a moment.*) Radio. Radio is. Oh. I can't believe that! Voices on the air, ladies! Sounds voodoo. You'll just have to osmose your own description.

(*Pause*)

MARY: We are imbued with the future.

(*Pause*)

FANNY: One doesn't have to like it.

(*Pause*)

MARY: Nostalgia for the future.

(*Pause*)

ALEX: I shall make my fortune in radio.

(*Pause*)

MARY: We shall go from year to year, as if we were going from tribe to tribe.

ALEX: Big fun!

(MARY *finds a button in the grass.*)

MARY: Look. Another button. Similar to the one we found our first day on the beach.

FANNY: "Hec—kwhod—ont"?

MARY: Once could be a fluke. Twice is a trend.

ALEX: What what what does the button read, Mary?

MARY: "I—Like—Ike".

(*Pause. Simultaneously:*)

MARY, ALEX, AND FANNY: Who's Ike?

(*They laugh. Pause.*)

FANNY: I don't know about all of you, but I do have a sudden craving. A burning desire. Intense, painful longing. (*Beat*) For "Cool Whip."

(*Pause*)

ALEX AND MARY: Hmmmmmmmm.

(*The ladies come downstage, grasp hands, and survey their prospects.*)

MARY: Ladies! Let us segue!

(*They disappear in a blaze of light.*)

Act Break

ACT TWO

(14) Fanmail from the Future

(The ladies are fording a stream, their skirts hiked up.)

FANNY: Ladies, we are in a strange new world. Where life as we know it is, well, not as we know it.

MARY: Treacherous underfoot. Careful on the bank.

ALEX: You will agree that trousers are eminently more sensible for situations like these.

MARY: Not at all.

FANNY: They'd be drenched. Damp for days at this altitude.

ALEX: You roll them up! You roll them up! You roll them up! You roll them up!

FANNY: Alexandra, collect yourself!

MARY: For all our sakes.

(They have reached the other side and unhike their skirts.)

ALEX: You cannot resist the future! It is futile! You must embrace it with all your heart!

FANNY: Alexandra. One has to accept the future. One doesn't have to embrace it.

ALEX: Pendejo!

MARY: Ladies, we are on the frontier of the future.

FANNY: I have always been a pioneer.

MARY: We have been encountering residue from the future. Flotsam from many different moments.

FANNY: "Fanmail" from the future.

MARY: What is "fanmail", Fanny?

FANNY: (*Osmosing*) Mash notes. Autographed glossies. Secret decoder rings.

MARY: Multiple mysteries!

(*A pathway of light. Objects appear in the air before them: a dazzling array of toys and junk and gadgets and souvenirs and appliances and electronic wonders, everything from an acid-pink hula hoop to a silver laser video disc.*)

(*The ladies gasp, delighted.*)

FANNY: "Fallout" from the future!

(*They begin to examine the objects, oooing and murmuring and clucking.*)

(FANNY *tries to osmose an odd toy.*)

FANNY: "Tweezer"! No. "Yo-yo"! No. "Mr. Coffee"! No. My osmos is not quite right.

(ALEX *follows suit.*)

ALEX: "Slot machine." "Juke box." "Squirt gun." "Brass knuckles."

(FANNY *finds a magazine.*)

FANNY: A tabloid "*The National Review*". (*She puts it in her pack.*)

ALEX: "Ovaltine." "Bosco." "Double Bubble." "Velvee-eeta."

MARY: A rain forest of fossils from the future.

ALEX: Oh, look! A mini-dirigible! (*She reads the fine print on an inflatable banana.*) "Not to be used as a life preserver." Hmmmm.

(FANNY *peers into a side-view mirror from an automobile.*)

FANNY: "Objects in mirror may be closer than they appear"? Hmmmm. Well, Mary, here is your physical evidence. What do you make of it?

MARY: Ladies. We have the artifacts—

(*They hold up their artifacts, including egg beaters and buttons.* FANNY *and* ALEX *have been wearing their egg beaters like pistols.*)

MARY:—we must find their historical moment. Let us camp tonight in this—orchard of the future. Tomorrow we shall enter fully the era that awaits us.

FANNY: I hope with all my heart I shall be able to have a bath. And find a post office.

(ALEX *points at* MARY'*s Ike button.*)

ALEX: Ladies, let us not forget. "Ike" is waiting.

(FANNY *and* ALEX *rotor at one another.*)

JOURNAL ENTRY:

> MARY: We spent the night in the future. Around us swirled a silent storm of images, a star shower of light from a new world.

(15) The Starry Deep

(*A starry night falls. The ladies pitch a gossamer canopy. They light lanterns. They write in their journals, each by her own light.*)

ALEX: Under a calliope of stars. Below the firmament. The glittering empyrean. The night above the dingle starry. (*Beat*) That's not mine. Damn this interference. (*Beat*) The vasty deep. The starry deep. (*Beat*) Under welkin.

MARY: Difficult to hack one's way through this thicket of voices from the future.

FANNY: Grover, my tender parsnip—shall I ever see you again?

MARY: Notes for a paper for the Boston Geo. I have tentatively dubbed this phenomenon we are experiencing—chronokinesis. (*Beat*) Fanny's tabloids will call it "time travel."

FANNY: Time travel is a tricky business, dear Grover. Beyond our ken.

MARY: Chronokinesis! Life membership in the Boston Geo. The Academy of Arts and Sciences. Honorary membership in the Royal Geo and Academie Française. Director of the Smithsonian. The first woman. The Nobel Prize in physics—

ALEX: My fellow polytopians are splendid and intrepid. Mary is excessively anecdotal, and Fanny scorns my lyrics.

FANNY: Mary and Alexandra are quite sweet, really. Appalling politics. Appalling. If we are detained in this country, I shall order them both a subscription to *The National Review*. I am quite certain you would adore *The National Review*, Grover. I do. It is the sole thing I've so far discovered in the future which reminds me of the nineteenth century.

ALEX: I foresee the day—it is exceedingly easy to foresee the day here—I foresee the day Fanny will eat her words. I shall secure an exclusive recording contract with a multinational conglomerate, and make consecutive gold records. (*Beat*) Note: meditate and osmose what those things are, exactly.

FANNY: The possibility exists that we shall not return, dear Grover. Certainly—in the northern hemisphere—one cannot simply go back and forth in time as one pleases. Time is not a revolving door. We have access to the future here. Do we have egress as well?

ALEX: We are beseiged by a barrage of fact. From here the future looks—

MARY: The future looks—

ALEX: The future looks positively—AMERICAN.

FANNY: Loud—

MARY: —invigorating. Quite promising, except, perhaps, for the theatre—which threatens to degenerate into imitations of anthropological kinship studies.

FANNY: We ought to be approaching a post office. Of course, it is a verity that the tropical post will forever be a sink of inefficiency, world without end.

ALEX: I expect to publish these memoirs with an insert of Kodak reproductions. I adore Kodaking.

FANNY: Can the post office deliver to you, in 1889, a letter from me—some decades later? I know they can do it the other way 'round. That's commonplace.

MARY: I for one am looking forward to meeting this "Ike." "Ike" "Ike" "Ike." "Iko Iko." "Willy and the Hand Jive."

FANNY: Beyond our ken, dear Grover. Trust you are staying dry. All my love. From Terra Incognita to Terre Haute. Fanny.

(*As* MARY *and* FANNY *sleep,* ALEX *comes down and does her journal entry.*)

ALEX: (*Taking a deep breath*) The rare air of the future. Breathe. Aspirate. Aspire. A—spire. (*She takes another deep breath.*) One of the ecstacies of hiking in the Himalayas was to crest a ridge, and suddenly confront the infinite surround. Mountains and rivers without end. Untouched. Glistening with possibility. We are climbing a spire of time. The topography of the future is coming into view. Unmapped and unnamed. Distant vistas shining. You must not shrink. You must embrace it with all your heart.

(16) Manna from Heaven—or, Among the Jesuits

(*Dawn. The ladies stir, take down the gossamer canopy.*)

FANNY: I slept not a wink.

MARY: Nor I.

ALEX: Nor I.

MARY: Fascinating as fire imagery. I long to learn more about "Willy and the Hand Jive."

FANNY: From what little I could fathom, the future seems a dubious prospect.

ALEX: (*A sudden transmission*) Beep!

FANNY: I beg your pardon.

ALEX: Wrong!

FANNY: Are you contradicting me, young lady?

ALEX: College bowl! State for twenty! The future is not a dubious prospect! The future is—just a bowl of cherries!

FANNY: Mary, we must locate a translator. Alexandra will soon be totally incomprehensible.

ALEX: Fanny, the future is now!

FANNY: Alexandra. (*Sighs*) I would elude the future, if I could.

ALEX: Fanny, you must embrace it with all your heart.

FANNY: Why? Why why why why why?

ALEX: Fanny, you sound like a broken record, a busy signal, a car alarm—

FANNY: Alexandra! (*Beat*) I must accept the future, Alexandra, as I accept the existence of cyclones and pit vipers and bad grammar. But you would have me embrace them?

ALEX: Yes!

FANNY: You would. Cyclones? Pit vipers? Bad grammar?

ALEX: In a way. Yes.

FANNY: You are a feckless child.

ALEX: And you, Fanny, you—are—so—so—so— SQUARE!

(*Pause*)

FANNY: I have seen the future. And it is slang.

(*Pause*)

MARY: It is uncommonly close this morning. I must put on a new face.

ALEX: I'll follow suit.

(MARY *and* ALEX *exit.*)

(FANNY *takes out her letter to* GROVER, *which has grown into a small volume. She calms herself by writing.*)

FANNY: Dearest Grover. Another addendum. As we home in on the future, I begin to feel curiously at ease, and happy. Content. We have been cantering along at a terrific clip. The future looms. (*Pause. She opens a music box. It plays.*) The future looms as steady and stable as a table top. I anticipate we shall find a year which suits me perfectly, and settle in for a long refreshment. I shall have a bath. There will be a post office. Oh, dear Grover—I feel we are on the verge of something grand.

(*An elegant gentleman in a beautiful white suit—*MR. COFFEE*—appears at the end of the path.* FANNY *is quite taken with him.*)

MR. COFFEE: Good afternoon, Madame.

FANNY: Sir.

(*He moves to her. He takes two cigarettes from a silver case, lights them, and gives one to her.*)

FANNY: Thank you. (*A little giddy*) And I don't even smoke. (*A sultry dual inhalation*) Oooo. In my day, Sir, a lady did not smoke tobacco.

MR. COFFEE: Modern times, Fanny, modern times.

FANNY: Too true.

MR. COFFEE: How are you finding your travels?

FANNY: Trying.

MR. COFFEE: Worth the candle?

FANNY: Without question. (*Beat*) Are you Mr. Coffee?

MR. COFFEE: I've been called worse.

FANNY: I've had a premonition about meeting you.

MR. COFFEE: I'm sure you have.

FANNY: You are not of this era.

MR. COFFEE: No. Not exclusively.

FANNY: Much too well spoken. Let me tell you, Mr. Coffee—language takes a beating in the future.

MR. COFFEE: And that goes double for diction. These things are cyclical, my dear. Do not despair. What goes around, comes around.

FANNY: Is that a local proverb?

MR. COFFEE: One of my favorites. An airmail letter?

FANNY: "Air-mail"? How funny. If you say so.

MR. COFFEE: (*Without looking*) Terre Haute, 1889. Airmail part of the way. Then Pony Express.

FANNY: (*Laughs*) Terre Haute is not Indian Territory, Mr. Coffee. This letter is a long-running serialization by now. I must mail it before the cost of postage becomes absolutely prohibitive.

MR. COFFEE: Preserve it for posterity. A fascinating memoir. You wouldn't want people to forget.

FANNY: Oh, no, it's much too long to copy. I suppose I could edit out the personal parts.

MR. COFFEE: If you venture on into the future, you'll eventually come across something called a Xerox.

FANNY: Oh, zeeroxen, I've seen those in Greenland.

(*Pause*)

MR. COFFEE: There is no hope of Grover ever receiving your letter, Fanny.

FANNY: The postal system is worrisome, Mr. Coffee, but not yet hopeless.

(*Pause*)

(FANNY *understands.*)

FANNY: Do you know Grover?

MR. COFFEE: We've met.

FANNY: Recently?

MR. COFFEE: Seems like only yesterday. But I have no sense of time.

FANNY: How was he? Was he dry?

MR. COFFEE: Dry as toast. Frankly, he's been better. Bit of a cough. His wife was not unduly concerned.

FANNY: I'm his wife.

MR. COFFEE: His second wife. He had you declared legally dead, dear. Terre Haute Superior Court, 1910.

FANNY: That man.

MR. COFFEE: Remarried a few years later.

FANNY: He never minded being alone when we were married.

MR. COFFEE: The Great War made him anxious. And wealthy.

FANNY: I thought those were new shoes. He came to me, Mr. Coffee. In a dream. (*Beat*) He told me not to speculate on the future.

MR. COFFEE: In his own brokerish fashion, Grover was trying to say—so long.

FANNY: So long. So long. (*Beat*) When did you last see Grover, Mr. Coffee?

MR. COFFEE: Our one and only meeting. October, 1929.

(*Pause*)

FANNY: How—?

MR. COFFEE: He hurled himself off the top of a grain silo.

FANNY: Oh, dear.

MR. COFFEE: Part of a gentle rain of brokers who fell from heaven that autumn all over the country.

FANNY: I've been out of touch.

MR. COFFEE: Grover was speculating on the commodities market. Blue sky ventures. You know. Futures.

FANNY: Blue sky ventures. Did he miss me?

MR. COFFEE: Very much, once he realized you were never coming home from Terra Incognita. Less and less, over the years. He'd get a little misty on the seminal holidays. Christmas. Easter. Arbor Day. Each and every Arbor Day he'd have three or four peppermint schnapps, in your memory, and plant a bush in the back yard. (*Beat*) At heart, he wasn't surprised you never returned from Terra Incognita. He'd always suspected you'd disappear one day. Vanish without a trace.

FANNY: Yes. He was always rather taken aback whenever I walked through the front door. Well. Thank you, Mr. Coffee.

MR. COFFEE: My pleasure.

FANNY: Tell me, Mr. Coffee. Do you find it easy to foresee the future?

MR. COFFEE: I've never had any trouble.

FANNY: No. I don't suppose you would.

MR. COFFEE: But I confine myself to the basics.

FANNY: We will meet again, I trust.

MR. COFFEE: I feel certain of it.

FANNY: But not for many years.

MR. COFFEE: You never know. (*He takes her hand.*)

FANNY: I have been wanting to speak to you.

MR. COFFEE: Yes. Here I am, after all. (*Kisses her hand.*) A bien tot.

FANNY: Vaya con Dios, Mr. Coffee.

MR. COFFEE: Charming. See you later. Alligator.

(*He exits. Passing* MARY *and* ALEX:)

MR. COFFEE: Ladies. (*He disappears.*)

MARY: Who on earth was that?

ALEX: (*Osmosing*) That was "Bebe Rebozo"!

FANNY: That was Mr. Coffee.

ALEX: Oh. Really. Sometimes this osmosing is wildly inaccurate.

MARY: The multiple possibilities of the future, dear. A man might be Mr. Coffee, or he might be Bebe Rebozo. What's his line?

FANNY: Prognostication. He had news. We're on the right track.

MARY: Splendid. Saddle up.

(ALEX *and* MARY *pick up their stuff and start off.*)

JOURNAL ENTRY:

> FANNY: (FANNY, *after a moment, silently folds the letter, tucks it away, and closes the music box.*)

(17) Vintage Crystal

(*Moonlight. A beautiful unearthly snow begins to fall.*)

ALEX: What is that?

FANNY: Snow. Unless I miss my guess.

ALEX: Cold and wet on the tongue. Melts right off.

FANNY: Snow it is.

ALEX: Like no snow I've known before.

FANNY: A new snow. A strange snow. An unknown snow.

MARY: Lambent. Luminous.

ALEX: Snow from the moon, ladies!

FANNY: Yes!

MARY: Yes! Lunar snow is not annoying!

(ALEX *catches snow and tastes.*)

JOURNAL ENTRY:

> ALEX: Lunar snow is, despite its apparent immaturity, a vintage precipitate. Coarser and sweeter than Himalayan, it stands up to all but the most robust Karakoram. Fruitier than Rocky Mountain powder, and a touch more acidic than Vermont sludge, it is altogether full-bodied and elusive. This is a young snow but not a callow snow, and should be confronted early—like the finest Hindu Kush—before the blush is off the slush, and the bloom is gone.

(18) Woody's Esso

(*Music:* "Rock Around the Clock" *playing on a radio. A gas pump and an Esso sign appear. Music fades out.*)

ALEX: Civilization.

MARY: The outskirts.

FANNY: How far our standards have fallen.

ALEX: If I were wearing trousers at this moment, I would change.

FANNY: (*An outburst*) You needn't suck up to me, Alexandra!

MARY: Fanny! Is that a vulgarity?

(*A pause*)

FANNY: I am sorry, Alexandra. I plead the future.

ALEX: I understand.

FANNY: You needn't mollify me, is what I meant. It seems to me that you were right.

ALEX: How nice. About what, dear Fanny?

FANNY: Trousers. Trousers trousers trousers. It seems clear to me that everyone in the future wears 'em. I am so glad I shan't live to see it. Of course, I am seeing it. I am so flummoxed. I wonder if we will remember all this when we return home.

MARY: If we return home.

(*A palanquin, with its shades drawn, rolls on. On it, a sign: The Dragon Lady, Fortunes Told, Palms Read, Charts, Crystal Ball, Tarot Cards, Etc.*)

MARY: I know what that is—

ALEX: A "hot rod."

MARY: A palanquin.

FANNY: Honestly, Alexandra, how quickly you've forgotten our own era.

MARY: Do you realize that palanquin is now an antique?

FANNY: So are we, my dear, so are we.

MARY: But what is it doing here? (*Indicates gas pump*) And what is that? And who is The Dragon Lady?

FANNY: Warrants investigation.

(*They start forward. A hand with long painted fingernails pulls back the shade suddenly, startling the ladies. It is* MADAME NHU, *who is wearing a beautiful if slightly ferocious half-mask. The eyes of the mask are Asian, the cheekbones high, and she wears a wig of long, jet-black hair. The effect is at once feminine and frightening. She looks them over. Her voice is low (not falsetto), and she speaks with a slight accent, both French and Asian.*)

MME. NHU: Come closer. Let me scrutinize you.

(*They approach cautiously.* MME. NHU *holds up a hand. They stop. After a moment, she begins to speak.*)

MME. NHU: Serious trouble will pass you by. Your mind is filled with new ideas—make use of them. He who does not accept cash when offered is no businessman. You are worrying about something that will never happen. Your talents will be recognized and suitably rewarded. You will never need to worry about a steady income. Soon you will be sitting on top of the world. The night life is for you. Praise your wife, even if it frightens her. You have an unusual equipment for success, be sure to use it properly. Be as soft as you can be and as hard as you have to be. Someone is speaking well of you. A new diet or exercise program can be unusually beneficial for you now. An unpleasant situation will soon be cleared to your satisfaction. Read more fine books and better magazines. Avoid fried foods, which angry up the blood. Let them eat barbecue!

(*A pause*)

(*The ladies look at one another.*)

(MME. NHU *thrusts out a plate with three fortune cookies on it. They each take a cookie.*)

MME. NHU: Let me tell you secret. The future is now. (*She pulls the shade and disappears.*)

ALEX: That was an image.

MARY: An oracle.

FANNY: An inscrutable pancake.

ALEX: What are these? (*Osmoses*) "Fortune cookies"!

MARY: No smell.

FANNY: No taste.

ALEX: Edible?

FANNY: Definitely not.

MARY: (*Breaks hers open.*) Inside—a scrap of paper.

ALEX: (*Likewise*) A message.

FANNY: (*Likewise*) Fanmail from some flounder.

(*They read their messages.*)

ALEX: You will become rich and famous.

FANNY: You will meet a tall dark stranger.

MARY: You will go on a long journey.

ALEX: This is exhilarating!

(*She approaches the palanquin, steps on an invisible rubber-tube gas station bell. It chimes: ding-dong, ding-dong.*)

(*A sign flies in: Woody's Esso.*)

(*GUS, a fresh-faced American teenager, appears, wearing a baseball cap and chewing gum. Boundless energy.*)

GUS: Hi! What'll it be? Hey! Wow! Gosh! Hello!

FANNY: Greetings, young man, from President Mc-Taft.

GUS: Swell feathers and fancy duds! You ladies look kinda like Kitty! Golly! You goin' to the prom or what! Gosh!

ALEX: Kitty?

GUS: Didja watch *Gunsmoke* last night? Or *Cimarron City*?

ALEX: Kitty?

GUS: Kitty see she runs the saloon and she's in love with Marshal Dillon who's the sheriff but he'll never marry her 'cause he's a bachelor—see *Bachelor Father*?

FANNY: My dear boy, a bachelor father is a paradox. An oxymoron. A contradiction in terms.

ALEX: Ladies—the future.

FANNY: (*Snorts*) Bachelor father. Mary, you have found your niche. Your prurient interest in anthropological smut should stand you in good stead. Bachelor father.

MARY: Oh, Fanny. Let us introduce ourselves.

ALEX: I'm Alexandra. This is Mary—

MARY: Hello, young man.

ALEX: And this is Fanny.

GUS: Hi! Hi! Hi! I'm Gus!

ALEX: Good afternoon, Gus.

GUS: Great! Wow, you ladies are kooky, no offense.

ALEX: How nice of you to say so.

FANNY: Gus, we are so very pleased to meet you. You are the first person we have encountered in our travels with a reasonable accent and an acceptable demeanor.

GUS: Lucky for me, huh? You ladies broke down somewhere? I don't see your eggbeater. Say, who do you like in the Series? The Dodgers or the Yanks?

(*Pause. Finally*, ALEX *smiles sweetly and says judiciously:*)

ALEX: Whom do you like?

GUS: I like the Dodgers.

ALEX: Then so do I.

GUS: Great!

MARY: Gus, dear, tell us about the palanquin.

ALEX: About the Dragon Lady.

MARY: A lady of ferocious aspect.

GUS: Madame Nhu.

ALEX: Madame Who?

GUS: Madame Nhu. She rents a parking space from Woody.

MARY: How did Madame Nhu and her palanquin happen to land here?

GUS: Just showed up one day. Out of the blue.

FANNY: Gus, dear, what year is it?

GUS: You don't know?! Come off it.

ALEX: We do not know. Honestly. It's hard to explain.

GUS: 1955. Everybody knows that.

ALEX: We don't.

GUS: Gee, I'm sorry. I'd give you a calendar—(*Blushes*) but they're not for girls. (*Beat*) Hey, you guys are kidding me. Huh? Huh? Come on, lay off. Just 'cause I'm a teenager.

MARY: What's a teenager?

FANNY: What's an Esso?

GUS: Esso is service, parts and dependability. So you're tourists, huh? I thought you had to be, I woulda remembered *you*.

MARY: Travelers, not tourists.

ALEX: Polytopians. Travelers to many lands.

FANNY: Charting the unknown.

MARY: Geography, cartography, ethnology, and the natural sciences.

GUS: Great. I could use a vacation myself. You need anything? Soda, gum, roadmaps, oil? Chiclets?

ALEX: I would like a "Chiclet", please.

GUS: Take two, they're small.

(GUS *gives* ALEX *some Chiclets. She examines them, pops them into her mouth, and chews.*)

GUS: Where you ladies from?

MARY: We are traveling through time, Gus.

GUS: You dames are some kidders. No? You mean it? You're on the level? Wow! Like you're from another

time?! Another dimension?! PARALLEL UNI-
VERSE?! Wait'll I tell my Dad! I saw this show—(*Beat
as he looks them over.*) Wow, so this is how they dress
in history! Gee! Do you wanna come to my social
studies class? So, do you believe in UFOs?

ALEX: Chiclets are sweet and tough, like dried manioc.

FANNY: Ah, Gus. We are looking for someone. Perhaps
you know him.

ALEX: Ike.

MARY: Perhaps you've heard of him.

GUS: Ike who?

ALEX: We do not know his surname.

MARY: We found his name on this button.

GUS: Nicky might know. He knows everybody.

(MARY *hands* GUS *the button.*)

GUS: Ho ho.

FANNY: You know this Ike.

GUS: Yeah, sure I know this Ike. Hangs out at the
station. Wants to be a grease monkey in his spare time.
I'm showing him the ropes. You guys. Whatta buncha
kidders.

ALEX: You don't know him?

GUS: My dad voted for him. Come on. What are ya,
gonna vote for that other clown, the Chicago egghead?
"I Like Ike." Great.

ALEX: Do you like Ike, Gus?

GUS: My dad likes him! I betcha Nicky knows this
Ike. 'Sides, you wanna stay there while you're in Peligrosa, doncha? Hold on, let me draw you a map. (*He
disappears.*)

ALEX: Mary! Fanny! Facts!

FANNY: Chronological and geographical. We are in
Peligrosa!

MARY: In the vicinity of 1955!

ALEX: Perhaps 1955 is the apotheosis of the future!

FANNY: This Ike must be a local Poobah!

ALEX: We shall palaver.

(GUS *reappears, with a map.*)

GUS: Okay, dokey, here's directions to Nicky's.

MARY: Is it far?

GUS: Just a hop skip and a jump. We're giving these away with a full tank. But for you guys—it's on the house.

(GUS *hands* MARY *an egg beater of yet a third design.*)

MARY: Marvelous! A matched set!

ALEX: Ladies! Whip them out!

(FANNY *and* ALEX *whip out their egg beaters. They all rotor and laugh. From this point on, the* LADIES *always wear their eggbeaters.*)

GUS: You collect 'em?!? I'd give you green stamps, but Woody'd kill me if—

FANNY: Gus, dear, does this Nicky fellow have a bath?

GUS: Nicky's—are you kidding? Does he have a bath? Are you kidding? He's got everything! He'll probably put you up. Wait'll you see the set-up at Nicky's. You are gonna flip!

FANNY: Hooper Do! (*She grabs the map.*) Gus, my undying devotion. Ladies—dog my heels.

ALEX: Adieu, Gus.

GUS: See you later, alligator.

MARY: Thank you, Gus. Perhaps we'll pass this way again.

GUS: After awhile, crocodile.

MARY: Ah, Gus! The Mighty Silurian!

GUS: Whatever you say, lady. Give Nicky some skin for me.

MARY: Whatever you say, Gus.

(GUS *exits.*)

(*Traveling music throbs: The theme from* Peter Gunn. *The ladies travel. They reach a spot, and huddle around a map.*)

MARY: X marks the spot.

(Peter Gunn *fades away.*)

ALEX: Have we misread it?

FANNY: Impossible. But perhaps we've passed it.

ALEX: My eyes were peeled.

FANNY: In time. Perhaps we've passed it in time. Perhaps it was here once. But now it's gone.

MARY: I think not. I have an unshakable conviction we have come to the center of 1955.

ALEX: Smack dab in the middle.

MARY: Well said, Alex.

FANNY: If the map's right, and the time's right, where the devil is this Nicky fellow? I'll horsewhip anyone who stands between me and a hot bath.

ALEX: I broke up a knife fight with a whip once. Oh, yes I did. Two sherpas were vying for a place by the fire.

(*Strains of Big Band music.*)

MARY: Do you hear that music?

FANNY: A mynah bird escaped from a cocktail lounge.

ALEX: Fanny, you redefine pessimism. What is a "cocktail lounge"?

FANNY: Osmose it yourself.

ALEX: (*Osmosing*) "Happy Hour"!

(*A loud burst of Big Band music.*)

MARY: Ladies—I believe we're on the verge!

(*All three ladies do journal entry in unison.*)

ALEX, MARY, AND FANNY: We arrive in '55!

(19) Paradise '55

(*Lights! A flashy sign, neon:* NICKY's. *Some palm trees and streamers: A gaudy, prerevolutionary Havana-style nightclub.*)

(NICKY *rolls on with a piano and live mike. Does a splashy finish.*)

NICKY: Vaya! Vaya! Vaya! Con! Dios! Wo Wo Wo Wo Wo—yeaaaaaah! Pow!

(*The ladies applaud.*)

NICKY: You're too kind.

(*Checks them out.*)

NICKY: My my my my my my my. Holy cow. What have we here. Our humble joint. Nicky's Peligrosa Paradise Bar and Grill. Graced by style, beauty, pulchritude and wit. Hi, I'm Nicky Paradise. Welcome to paradise—where hospitality still means something.

ALEX: (*Instantly smitten*) O brave new world, that has such creatures in it!

FANNY: Alex, you are a terrible plagiarist.

MARY: Instantly smitten.

NICKY: Make yourselves at home. (*His best smile*) Mi casa es su casa! (*Reprise—best smile*) My house is your house. Toss back a coupla stiff ones, grab a bite, cool out in the casino, catch a show, let your hair down, loosen your corsets—

MARY, FANNY, AND ALEX: Mr. Nicky!

NICKY: Please. Nicky.

ALEXANDRA: Alexandra Cafuffle.

FANNY: Mrs. Cranberry. You may call me Fanny.

NICKY: It would break my heart if I couldn't.

MARY: Mary Baltimore. From Boston.

NICKY: Such tropicana, such feminality. Overwhelmed, truly.

(*He dashes to the piano and plays and sings a phrase of* "Bad Boy.")

NICKY: "I'm just a bad boy-oy-oy-oy-oy-oy-oy-oy-oy-oy-oy—
  All dressed up in fancy clothes
  I am takin' the trouble
  To blow all my bubbles away."

ALEX: Mr. Paradise!

NICKY: Nicky.

FANNY: Mr. Paradise—

NICKY: Nicky, Nicky, Nicky!

FANNY: Nicky, Nicky, Nicky. I hope you won't think me indelicate—

NICKY: Never.

FANNY: —but I simply must have a scrub immediately. Post haste. It's been eons. Can you arrange for me to have a bath?

NICKY: For you, Fanny—a whirlpool. (*He snaps his fingers and plays the piano. A light appears.*) Follow that light, Fanny. Don't be stingy with the bubbles. That's what they're there for.

FANNY: Bubbles. I won't ask. I'll just hold my nose and dive in. Ladies.

(*She exits.*)

(NICKY *sings and plays after her:* "Vaya Con Dios My Darling/Vaya Con Dios My Love.")

MARY: Nicky's Peligrosa Paradise Bar and Grill?

NICKY: Be there or—(*Smiles his best smile*) be square.
(MARY *holds out her button.*)

MARY: Perhaps you can shed some light.

NICKY: Oh yeah. I like Ike. Who doesn't?

MARY: Who don't?

NICKY: Have it your way, Mary. I'm easy.

MARY: I like Ike. Heck, who don't?

NICKY: Hardly anybody.

(MARY *pulls out the original button she found on the beach.*)

MARY: Indeed. "Heckwhodon't?" Heck—who—don't. It's a companion button. I like Ike. Heck, who don't?

NICKY: You're sharp. Need a job?

ALEX: Brava, Mary! I love a good mystery, don't you?

(MARY *pins the buttons on* ALEX.)

MARY: Do you know him? Gus said you might.

ALEX: We would very much like to meet him.

MARY: He has become a point of some interest with us.

ALEX: Do you know this Ike?

NICKY: We're like this. Never vacations anywhere but Nicky's. He and Mamie are nuts about the joint. He's gonna make Nicky's a national monument.

ALEX: Is he in residence at present?

NICKY: Yeah, he's in back, smoking a cigar. I'll take you around.

ALEX: Oh, goody. I'll Kodak him for posterity!

NICKY: You'll like Ike. Everybody does. He's a likeable guy. Plays a fair round of golf. No duffer, Ike. You play?

MARY: The Scottish game? No. Speaking of games, am I correct in understanding that there is a gambling emporium on the premises?

NICKY: The casino. First rate. Slap a little blackjack, shoot some craps, spin the wheel, pull some slots, float a check. Whatever.

MARY: Gambling provides a fascinating study in cross-cultural comparisons. For instance, did you know that the Ute Indians of the American West are avid gamblers, and will wager their life's possessions on a single throw of the dice?

NICKY: No, I did not know that. Did you know that the Nevada looney bins are full of catatonic blue-haired ladies going like this? (*He demonstrates: catatonic slot-machine addicts plus sound effects.*)

MARY: No, I did not. Fascinating. I do not indulge, personally, of course, but with your permission, I should like to take notes.

(NICKY *hands her some chips.*)

NICKY: Have a ball, Mar'—knock yourself out.

(*He snaps his fingers, plays the piano. A light appears.*)

MARY: Not annoying! (*She follows the light. As she is about to exit, she turns;*) Ah, Nicky. Gus said to give you some of his skin.

NICKY: Thanks, doll.

(*She exits.* NICKY *plays, sings after her:* "There Goes My Baby/Movin' On Down the Line.")

(*He turns his attentions to* ALEX)

NICKY: Great kid, Gus.

ALEX: He drew us a map. That is how we located you.

NICKY: No, it's not.

ALEX: I beg your pardon.

NICKY: I said, that's not how you came to Nicky's, Al.

ALEX: Are you contradicting me?

NICKY: It wasn't a map that brought you to me, Al. It was—(*Best smile*) Kismet.

ALEX: I don't understand.

NICKY: You were destined to come to Nicky's.

ALEX: Perhaps you're right. I do have a positive feeling about 1955. It's—it's—it's—*keen*!

NICKY: I'm having a great year. So you stopped at Woody's. See the Dragon Lady?

ALEX: Madame Nhu?

NICKY: Madame Nhu. She's usually parked out front, filing her foot-long nails.

ALEX: Lovely palanquin.

NICKY: Isat what it is? I thought it was a chopped Chevy. Ike should be done with his cigar now. Want to meet him?

ALEX: Desperately.

(NICKY *snaps his fingers plays the piano. A light.*)

NICKY: Second door on the right. Knock three times. If Mamie answers, come back. We'll do it later.

ALEX: At long last, Ike! I'm off to meet the Ike! Ta! Ike get a kick out of you! Ike, can't get you out of my mind!

NICKY: Hold your hula hoops! Al, you aren't, by any chance, a lyricist?

ALEX: How did you guess?

NICKY: I can spot talent! I could use a good word jockey. Meet me in the lounge later. We'll pen some tunes. I have a lucrative new contract to script some billboards for Burma Shave.

ALEX: Fantastic! I've been dying to know what Burma Shave is.

NICKY: Al, I told you. Kismet.

ALEX: Ike can't get no satisfaction!

(*She exits. As* NICKY *styles on the piano* FANNY *enters, resplendent and transformed in 50's cocktail dress and blonde wig, still wearing eggbeater.*)

NICKY: Holy smokes! I have not seen duds like that since *High-School Confidential.*

(*He sweeps* FANNY *off her feet.*)

NICKY: What do you say we trip the light fantastic?

(*They do a slow romantic dance to Duke Ellington's* Dual Highway, NICKY *showing* FANNY *some sharp moves.* FANNY *grows more confident with every step. By the end of the dance, they are falling in love. They finish the dance and go to the table.*)

NICKY: Fred and Ginger have nothing on us—nothing! (*Gets intimate.*) Say, do you remember those little Danny Boone hats with the wacky raccoon tails?

FANNY: I'm afraid not.

NICKY: They were a gas. How was the whirlpool?

(*After a sensuous pause,* FANNY *says:*)

FANNY: Wow—wow—wow! Captivating. All those little jets of water were—quite—mesmerizing. I feel light-headed. Swoozy all over. (*Beat*) Jacuzzi all over.

NICKY: I don't follow you.

FANNY: Your whirlpool is called a jacuzzi. Or will be.

NICKY: I like the sound of that. Jacuzz'.

FANNY: Your establishment is uncanny. A veritable pleasure dome.

NICKY: I like to think of it that way.

(*She pulls out one of her postcards.*)

FANNY: It's just like my postcard.

NICKY: Hey! Where did you get this? These are sharp!

FANNY: I brought it with me. It's a postcard from the future. Of Nicky's. The view come true! Generic nightspot.

NICKY: Like I always say, Fanny—the future is now. I'm gonna put 'em in all the rooms with the Gideon Bibles.

FANNY: Mister Paradise—

NICKY: Hey, I'm gonna get cross wit' you—

FANNY: Nicky. Since we've been in the vicinity of 1955, there's something I've had a craving for—

NICKY: Please. Say no more.

(*He prestidigitates a huge glass goblet and two spoons. As* FANNY *closes her eyes*—)

FANNY: I am agog with anticipation.

(*He holds the goblet under her nose. She inhales deeply, with ecstasy, and slowly opens her eyes.*)

FANNY: Cool Whip!

NICKY: The Real McCoy.

(*He hands her a spoon. They each dish out a spoonful of Cool Whip. They lock eyes. They lock arms, as though drinking champagne. They raise the spoons to their lips.*)

NICKY: Here's to you—Fanny.

(*They clink spoons. They take a bite. A dazzled pause.*)

FANNY: Oh! good!

(*Freeze. Music swells.* NICKY *and* FANNY *exit.*)

(ALEX *enters and does journal entry.*)

> ALEX: (*Formally, still, a bit out of rhythm, and trying to snap her fingers, perhaps using* NICKY'S *mike.*)
> On the go or at the beach
> After hours or safe at home
> For a cheek as smooth as a Georgia peach
> You need the shave that's like a poem—
> Burma Shave!

(20) Later That Same Evening

(ALEX *moves to the table and examines Cool Whip.*)

ALEX: (*Osmoses*) "Mo hair". No. "Jello mold". No. (*Tastes*) Noxzema! Yes! Heaven!

(MARY *enters, to a swirl of music, tipsy and exhilarated.*)

MARY: I have experienced an epiphany in the casino. I beat the one-armed bandit, kid! As they say here in 1955. Look!

(*She pours a cascade of nickles out of her helmet onto the table.*)

ALEX: Fantastic! I love the future!

MARY: And how did you do, Alexandra? Did you run the elusive Ike to ground? Tree him? Beard him in his lair?

ALEX: Mamie answered.

MARY: You'll collar him tomorrow. Quite a card, Ike. Una tarjeta, en español. Not many people know that.

ALEX: And how do you know that?

MARY: A bulletin from the future.

ALEX: What else does your bulletin tell you about Ike?

(MARY *osmoses.*)

MARY: He is a poobah of the first water. Golf clubs. Cardigan sweaters. (*Rubs her head.*) Cue ball.

ALEX: Cue ball?

MARY: (*With great dignity*)
"He has got a cue ball head that is hard as lead—
But he is all right with me.
Wo wo."

ALEX: Mary.

MARY: It is extraordinary what blossoms in one's brain in this country. That is from something called— (*Osmoses*) "Rock and roll."

ALEX: "Rock and roll." . . . Whomp bop a lula a wombat too!

(*She then scats the guitar part to the Surfari's WI-PEOUT!, doing 50's rock moves, and ending with a big finish.*)

ALEX: Wombat!

MARY: My. Osmosing the future is far more strenuous than navigating the upper reaches of the Congo.

ALEX: The January 1955 *Variety* magazine says rock and roll will be gone by June. Oh! What month are we?

MARY: I've no idea.

ALEX: I hope it's not June. I am dieting to rock and roll. I mean determined. Not dieting.

MARY: Hello, what's this? Manioc? (*She takes a spoonful of Cool Whip.*)

ALEX: Noxzema.

MARY: Have you tried it? (*She smears some on her face.*)

ALEX: Mmm. The texture is indescribable.

MARY: (*Takes a big bite—savors*) Why, this is sheer heaven, Alexandra.

(FANNY *floats on, now in a tight evening dress, looking blowzy and wonderful, still wearing her eggbeater.*)

FANNY: More than sheer heaven, Mary. Paradise.

ALEX: You look the cat that swallowed the canary.

FANNY: We were dancing!

ALEX: Really.

FANNY: Nicky is a divine dancer.

ALEX: Have some Noxzema.

FANNY: Cool Whip!

ALEX: Oh!

MARY: So this is Fanny's Cool Whip!

FANNY: Luscious, isn't it? I had the most extraordinary experience earlier this evening in a celestial contraption called a jacuzzi.

MARY: You should have seen the ecdysiastical "floor show" in the casino. The natives call it *Girls A Poppin'!* As fascinating as fire. From an anthropological point of view. Reminiscent of the vernal fertility rites in Sumatra, which always culminated in a riot of gymnastic—

FANNY: Mary, spare us your salacious anthropological details.

MARY: Remarkably supple. A cornucopia of concupiscence.

ALEX: Ladies—get a load of this! I am osmosing jingles like crazy! (*She licks a finger, presses it to her hip, makes a sizzling sound, and uses* NICKY's *mike.*)
Okay, tiger, striped and brave
A close clean scrape is what you crave
To fashion's whim you are no slave
You take it off—with Burma Shave!

FANNY: Wow! Wow! Wow!

ALEX: Jingles are the art form of the future!

FANNY: Why do they call it Burma Shave? What's it got to do with Burma?

MARY: I've been to Burma.

FANNY: As have I.

ALEX: The future is not dull!

FANNY: This is not the future, Alexandra. This is 1955.

MARY: Not annoying!

FANNY: Not bad! And that jacuzzi is really something.

(ALEX *dishes out a spoonful of Cool Whip. The others follow suit.*)

ALEX: To the future!

MARY: To us!

ALEX: To yetis and dirigibles—

FANNY: Jacuzzis—

MARY: To our adventures, many more!

ALEX: And here's to the elusive Ike!

(*They all clink spoons.*)

ALL: Cheers! Ike!

(*They all take a bite. A dazzled pause.*)

ALL: Oh, good!

(*Lights change.* FANNY *and* ALEX *exit.* MARY *comes downstage and does her journal entry.*)

> MARY: The pleasures of Nicky's Peligrosa Paradise Bar and Grill were—philharmonic. I blossomed into—I almost blush to recall it— a bonafide voluptuary, sampling an assortment of what were called, in the native parlance, 'leisure-time activities'. Re-creation. The casino was an anthropologist's field day, an anthology of human mis-demeanor. It's fascinating as fire floorshow, *Girls-A-Poppin'!*, held, I felt, the key to the culture, and was worth years of intense scrutiny. Television proved an addictive, if ultimately incomprehensible, hypnotic. And I thought the jacuzzi the greatest piece of engineering since the wheel. In short, I went, as the topical lingo had it, on a "bender." (*Beat*)
>
> The Byzantine pleasures of Nicky's intoxicate—but do not satiate. I flash and yearn for adventures beyond the jacuzzi.

(21) Go-Go Boots—or, Rock and Roll Is Here To Stay

(FANNY *and* ALEX *enter. It is some months later:* FANNY *is wearing a sensible 50's sun dress and* ALEX *is dressed*

in pedal pushers, carrying a surfboard. FANNY *has a
picnic basket and cooler. Both wear eggbeaters.*)

ALEX: (*To* FANNY) I've yet to catch a glimpse of him.
That Mamie guards him like a gryphon.

FANNY: Perhaps Ike is a yeti.

ALEX: Mary—look what I found! Surfboard!

MARY: What is the cultural application of a surfboard, Alexandra?

ALEX: Hang ten. Shoot the pipeline. Curl the Big Ka-
huna.

MARY: Whatever you say, Alex.

(FANNY *pulls out a pair of white boots.*)

FANNY: Alexandra may have her surfboard, but I have
my "go-go boots". A white ceremonial shoe. Worn
while mashing potatoes, riding ponies, and palaver-
ing with the Watusi.

MARY: I've found a tile. (*She holds up a green tile.*)

FANNY: Terra cotta?

MARY: Congoleum.

FANNY: Congoleum. What's it got to do with the
Congo?

MARY: I know not.

FANNY: I've been to the Congo.

MARY: As have I.

ALEX: Mary, you are the ginchiest. Hang in there.

MARY: I shall. I shall hang in there. I owe you a great
debt, Alexandra.

ALEX: No prob, Mar'. No sweat. No skin off my nose.

FANNY: Alexandra. Only a moment in 1955, and already your language is beyond redemption.

ALEX: Loosen your living girdle, Fanny.

MARY: Ah, Alexandra, how are your jingles?

ALEX: I've given them up for rock and roll.

FANNY: A fleeting fad.

ALEX: Fanny, rock 'n roll is here to stay. So, when's the shindig?

MARY: Shindig?

FANNY: I believe she means the authentic suburban charred meat festival you promised us.

MARY: Ah, yes. The bar-be-cue.

ALEX: Yes, what are we having—barbecued manioc?

FANNY: I am so excited. I haven't set foot outside the Paradise since our arrival.

(MARY *picks up her pack, which is fully rigged out for trekking.*)

FANNY: Mary! Where on Earth is this picnic? You have enough gear for a trek.

MARY: I have discovered within myself a new world. A voluptuousness which astounds me with its magenta sunsets, its incarnadine passions, its indigo fevers, tropical storms, and throbbing scarlet heart. Having discovered my voluptuous inclination, I have no intention of leaving it unexplored. Ladies—the future beckons! Don't you see? What we all need is further adventures!

ALEX: Oh, Mary, yes!

FANNY: Might be nice. A few days' trek. See something of the hinterlands.

MARY: I had in mind going on.

ALEX: Oh, I don't want to go back.

MARY: Not back. On.

FANNY: I adore 1955. It would break my heart to leave. (*Beat*) I love this. The occasional barbecue. (*Beat*) Entre nous—we're engaged!

MARY AND ALEX: Oh, Fanny!

FANNY: Thank you. We are very happy. The night Nicky popped the question, I was agog with anticipation. Yes I said yes yes oh yes I will my mountain flower as well you as another my flower of Andalusia and the pink and blue and yellow houses—(*Stops herself*) Goodness.

ALEX: What will Grover say?

FANNY: Ah, Grover, dear Grover, my tender parsnip. Grover will have apoplexy. You know, I can scarcely recall what Grover looks like. His face is fading from my memory like a hand-tinted picture postcard. I never told you. Grover passed on in 1929. Did away with himself, poor dear. Despondent over pork belly futures.

MARY: Poor Fanny. How do you know?

FANNY: Mr. Coffee told me. That man. Did you know he had me declared legally dead?

ALEX: No!

MARY: Well, three cheers for you, Fanny. (*Turns to* ALEX) Alex? There are new worlds out there. Where the air is rare.

ALEX: I have a date. I'm writing tunes with the Gorge Troll. We've got an offer from the House O' Hits. They want to buy our new number, *Mind Your Own Beeswax*. Then we're going for a spin on his chopper. Now that I know what a chopper is.

(*Pause*)

MARY: It seems a shame to break up the team.

ALEX: You don't have to.

(*Pause*)

MARY: Perhaps we are meant to be solo sojourners after all.

(*Pause*)

FANNY: I'll go scout out a spot to fire up the briquets.

ALEX: I'll follow suit.

(*As they leave:*)

FANNY: Are you reading your subscription to *The National Review*?

ALEX: Troll and I are writing tunes. I haven't time for arcane political journals.

FANNY: Not arcane. Germane.

ALEX: That's not a true rhyme. But it's not bad.

FANNY: High praise.

(*They're gone.*)

(*Nicky's Peligrosa disappears as* MARY *comes downstage and does her journal entry.*)

> MARY: My brain is full of exhilirating bulletins. On the horizon, a transcendent light flashes off the spires of the future. This New World is a garden. Splendors and wonders, marvels and mysteries. Miracles which top even Cool Whip.

(22) The Geography of Yearning

(ALEX *enters, in motorcycle leathers.*)

ALEX: Nothing shall ever replace Cool Whip in my affections. So. You're really going?

MARY: Yes.

ALEX: Seems a shame.

MARY: I'm restless. Wanderlust. You know.

ALEX: I have a faint recollection. (*Beat*) I do feel a tug. But I belong here.

MARY: This is what you wanted. The Show Business.

ALEX: It's Kismet. Here in 1955 is my brilliant career. I am part of the entertainment industry.

MARY: Good for you.

ALEX: I am wanton.

MARY: Alex.

ALEX: I mean weepy. Not wanton.

(*They embrace.* FANNY *enters, dressed for bowling.*)

FANNY: You're still here. Thank goodness. Alexandra, what a get up.

(ALEX *shoots a look at* FANNY'S *own get-up.*)

MARY: Dear Fanny.

FANNY: I do have a bit of a hankering to hit the trail with you, old friend. But 1955 suits me. To a T-Bird. Nicky is such a—dancer.

MARY: Will you invite Ike to the wedding?

FANNY: Entre nous, he's Nicky's best man.

ALEX: Goody! I'll Polaroid him for posterity.

(NICKY *enters, also ready to bowl a few frames.*)

NICKY: Fan, you look sensational, doll. Al, I ran your latest lyric up the flagpole, and I saluted, sweetheart, Mar'.

MARY: Nick'.

NICKY: And I used to think you had no sense of humor.

MARY: Live and learn.

NICKY: I sure will. So, what's the word, thunderbird?

MARY: Mr. Nicky, your emporium is most enticing. The sirens seduce.

NICKY: They really wail, don't they?

MARY: But I have strapped myself to the mast, and must sail on.

NICKY: When you gotta go, you gotta go. (*He hands her a container of Cool Whip.*) A little pick-me-up for the open road. You're not gonna find a lot of St. Bernards with Cool Whip in their kegs. Happy trails.

MARY: Oh, Nicky. Congratulations.

NICKY: Fanny spilled the beans, huh?

MARY: I think so.

NICKY: Sorry you won't be here for the big day.

MARY: I shall be here in spirit.

NICKY: So long. Just remember the immortal words of Satchel Paige. Don't look back—something might be gaining on you.

MARY: Ah, the sage Satchel Paige. He also said, to keep the juices flowing, jangle around gently as you move.

NICKY: I'll keep it in mind.

MARY: Sound advice. I intend to follow it to the letter.

ALEX: Mary. Before you go. You must give us the lowdown on the future.

MARY: I've only had glimpses, mind you. Flashes. Bits of light.

(*She osmoses, uttering each new word as if it were being spoken for the very first time. Coining place names for a map of the New World:*)

MARY: Electric eyes. Automatic tellers. TV dinners. And that's just the beginning.

Trailer parks. Mobile homes. Home economics.

O! Revolving credit! Spinoffs. Tax shelters, subsidiary rights. Offshore banking. Venture capital. Residuals.

Non-dairy creamer. Non-profit foundations. No-fault insurance.

Pot stickers. Nehru jackets. Lava lamps. Day glo. Black light. The Peace Corps. Soul music. The Fab Four. Fern bars. Fondue. Free love. Romanian Cabernet Sauvignon.

Disposable income. Significant others. Mood elevators.

Mood rings. Mud wrestling. Super stars. Floating anchors. Guest hosts. Low riders.

Slam dancing. Soft ware. Prime time. Time sharing. Word processors. Double speak. Hyper space. Holograms.

Aura cleansing. Angelic intervention. Pace makers. Walk mans. Synthesizers. Ghetto blasters. 45's. Saturday night specials.

Pulsars. Fiber optics. Remote control. Double think. Think tanks. The Domino Theory. The Third World. Boat people. Heavy water. Enhanced radiation. Silly Putty. Patty melts. Melt down. Ground zero. Fellow travelers.

Windows of vulnerability.

(*Pause*)

FANNY: Fellow travelers, yes, yes, yes, yes, yes we are, yes!

ALEX: And vulnerable windows! Marvelous!

MARY: Ladies, what do you say we have one last rotor? Just—one for the road, as it were?

FANNY: Splendid idea.

(*Egg beaters appear.*)

FANNY: Ready?

ALEX: Set?

MARY: Rotor!

(*They rotor vigorously. A good long rotor and a good long laugh.*)

(*Finished,* MARY *steps downstage, whips off her long Victorian skirt—*)

ALEX: Mary!

FANNY: Nicky, don't look!

(—*With a flourish. Underneath, she is wearing trousers.*)

ALEX: Brava, Mary!

MARY: I told you, Alexandra, I owe you a great debt.

ALEX: Intrepid trekking. Perhaps our paths will cross again, at some caravanserai of the future.

MARY: I feel certain of it. Our parabolas will intersect once more.

(*Sound of an enormous unmuffled motorcycle pulling up outside.*)

ALEX: That's Troll. Gotta go. Ciao.

FANNY: Dig you on the flip side.

(*She exits. Motorcycle roars off.*)

MARY: Mr. Nicky, thank you for everything.

(*She shakes his hand, and turns it into a hip handshake.*)

NICKY: Hey, hey, hey—

MARY: (*Gives him a wink*) Willy and the Hand Jive.

NICKY: You're hip, Mar'.

MARY: You, Nick', are impertinent. Give Gus some skin for me.

NICKY: So long.

FANNY: See you later, alligator. Au revoir, bon voyage. Stay dry. Try to write. And look out for zeeroxen.

MARY: Goodbye, Fanny.

FANNY: Vaya con Dios.

(NICKY *and* FANNY *exit.*)

(MARY *saddles up and comes downstage.*)

MARY: The splash of galaxies across the night sky always brings out the phenomenologist in me.

(*The stars come out.*)

MARY: Billions of new worlds, waiting to be discovered. Explored and illuminated. Within and without. The nautilus shell mimics the shape of the Milky Way. Quarks and quasars. My face is bathed in light from a vanished star. (*Beat*) I stand on the precipice. The air is rare. Bracing. Before me stretch dark distances.

Clusters of light. What next? I have no idea. Many mysteries to come. I am on the verge.

(*She surveys the horizon and her prospects.*)

MARY: I have such a yearning for the future! It is boundless! (*She takes a deep breath.*) Not annoying. Not annoying at all!

(*She disappears in a blaze of light—*)

End of play

PRODUCTION NOTES

The author wishes to thank Peter Culman and Stan Wojewodski, Managing Director and Artistic Director of Center Stage, respectively, for their continuing support.

The language of the play, since it is, at least in part, a play *about* language, cannot, must not, should not be naturalized or paraphrased. Rhythm and sound are sense. "One tiny *Times'* item" is very different from "One tiny *Times'* article."

Simple, plain, unaffected American speech, please. If the words are decorated, oversung, or have English lacquered over them, they become arch, unbearable, precious.

This is a play about the imagination, and about theatricality. It should be conveyed imaginatively and theatrically, not literally—in other words, with light, movement, and sound.

The titles and journal entries separate the scenes. The actress speaks the journal entry directly to the audience while the others prepare for the next scene.

MARY is the oldest, the leader, a passionate scientist, ebullient, joyful, not dry or academic. She is from Boston, but does not affect a pronounced Boston accent.

FANNY is from the Midwest. She is conservative, and has a wry wit.

ALEX is the youngest. An apostle of the future, she is most modern, most out of place in the Victorian world. She has boundless energy.

Disclaimer
On the Verge is not a docu-drama. I first encountered the historical Victorian lady travelers in Evan S. Connell's *A Long Desire*, Luree Miller's *On Top of the World*, Alexandra Allen's *Traveling Ladies*, and Dorothy Mid-

dleton's *Victorian Lady Travelers*, beautiful books all, and there is currently a plethora of books about and by the lady travelers. Research about them should be done for insight into their spirit, and for the pleasure of it. The characters of the play are NOT modeled upon particular individuals, even though I have raided the historical record for detail, flavoring, and anecdote. The spirit of the lady travelers inspired *On the Verge*, and that spirit is the play's true concern: the quality of yearning, courage, and imagination.

Thanks to:

Ellie Huber, Alexandra Gersten, Nicky Paraiso, Paul Walker, New Writers At The Westside; Roberta Levitow, Peter Hackett, Peter Parnell; Sarah Chodoff, Beth Dixon, James F. Ingalls, Tony Straiges, Lisa Marfleet, Sally Livingston, Del Risberg, Timothy Monich, Victoria Nolan, Jean Brubaker, Susan Andrews, Barbara Robinson, Mary Layne, Marek Johnson, Janet Kallas, Warren MacIsaac, Center Stage; Madelaine Puzo, Bill Storm, Roger Trefousse, Paddy Edwards, Libby Boone, Susan Barnes, Gordon Davidson, Murray Hepner, Mark Taper Forum; Raul Moncada, Kent Dorsey, Bob Berlinger, Paul Frelich, Tom Hall; Jerry Turner, Demetra Pittman, Ursula Meyer, Marie Livingston, Douglas Markonnen, Jim Sale, Bill Bloodgood, Bill Patton, Jeannie Davidson, Oregon Shakespearean Festival; Michael Engler, Fran McDormand, Jean Passanante, Susan Rowlands; Jack Clay, Chris Rusch, John Rainone, Sharon Ulrick; Craig Latrell, Karen Gjelsteen, Katherine Ferrand, Linda Emond, Nathan Haas, Ki Gottberg, Richard Edwards, Burke Walker, Empty Space; Mark Lamos, Kate Burton, Laurie Kennedy, Pamela Payton-Wright, David Hawkanson, Dunya Ramicova, Robert Wierzel, Derek McLane, Candice Chirgotis, Hartford Stage Company; Peter Altman, Michael Masso, Christine Rose, Pamela Berlin, Huntington Theatre; Liviu Ciulei, Mike Steele, Hugh Landwehr, Pat Collins, Garland Wright, Mary Beth Fisher, Peggy Cowles, Andre Gregory, The Guthrie, Jennifer Harmon, Michael Tolaydo.

Apologies to those I've omitted or misspelled.

Special thanks to Brenda Wehle, Jim McDonnell, Arthur Hankett, Mark Bly, Michael Lupu, Steven Dansky, Kip Gould, Melissa Cooper.

Infinite gratitude to Stan Wojewodski and Peter Culman. Infinite gratitude^2 to Jackson Phippen, who influenced so much the shape of the play.